HOME RUN

The Reverse Mortgage Advantage

Steven Ranson
and Yvonne Ziomecki

 FriesenPress

Suite 300 - 990 Fort St
Victoria, BC, V8V 3K2
Canada

www.friesenpress.com

ISBN
978-1-5255-9929-3 (Hardcover)
978-1-5255-9928-6 (Paperback)
978-1-03-911560-6 (Paperback)
978-1-5255-9930-9 (eBook)

1. BUSINESS & ECONOMICS, PERSONAL FINANCE, RETIREMENT PLANNING

Distributed to the trade by The Ingram Book Company

CONTENTS

FOREWORD

BY STEVEN RANSON

Let me begin by first thanking you for picking up this book on reverse mortgages that my colleague Yvonne Ziomecki and I have spent the past months writing together. While you may think a book coming from a financial institution might be inherently dry and filled with "corporate speak," I want to assure you that isn't the case with this book. As you'll find out in the pages ahead, we're not your typical bank, and this isn't your typical book on reverse mortgages!

Before I dive into HomeEquity Bank's storied history and my experience being at the helm for more than two decades, I want to tell you about what makes our product unique, about the values we embrace and about why we've made a commitment to helping Canadians live out their retirement in the homes they love.

You may not know this, but we're the only Canadian bank solely focused on the needs of Canadian homeowners 55 years old and up. Canadians who are 55-plus are the fastest-growing demographic in the country, and their financial needs are as diverse as they are. Yet despite all their differences, the one thing that unites our clients is their desire to live out retirement in their own way.

Millions of Canadians have worked incredibly hard their entire lives: raising families, growing their careers and businesses, doing their very best to get ahead with the dream of being able to comfortably retire in the home they love for as long as possible. But as we all know, life rarely goes according to plan. The fact is, even the best thought-out retirement strategies aren't exempt from external factors that can significantly disrupt one's financial well-being. Not only that, but life expectancy is increasing, the rate of savings is declining, and dependable company pensions have become unicorns.

With all this in mind, there are few options out there for Canadian homeowners age 55 or older who need access to capital, especially those who have retired and don't have continuous income. Most don't have the option of going back to work, and with other financial institutions making it harder to be approved for a home equity line of credit, sadly many are forced to sell their home and downsize. This doesn't have to be the case.

That's where HomeEquity's CHIP Reverse Mortgage™ comes in—a product I firmly believe has changed many lives for the better. Unlike traditional mortgages, ours requires no monthly mortgage payments, providing you with full independence when it comes to how and where you choose to spend. Not only that, but the money you receive is tax-free and repayment of the loan is only required once you move or sell. But the biggest reason I'm incredibly proud of this product is that it enables retirees to keep full ownership of their home. To me, it's especially rewarding to lead an organization whose core mission is to help people stay in the homes they love and live a comfortable life.

Our entire organization from top to bottom cares deeply about our customers, and we are steadfast in our dedication to providing service that goes above and beyond what other financial institutions even come close to. We're a compassionate company that has launched a number of initiatives that let our customers know we care. Our company value of helping older Canadians live more comfortably in the homes they love speaks true to our character. For example, when the pandemic hit, we launched Operation Warm Hug, where employees across the bank, me included, reached out to nearly two thousand customers to let them know they were not alone when they were forced to self-isolate.

We've also donated and worked with charities such as the YMCA of Greater Toronto (where I sit on the board) as well as the Canadian Red Cross and others, to give back to the community. I'm a big believer in giving back, and HomeEquity's philanthropic and volunteer efforts are a key part of our identity as an organization. Whether we're helping Canadians age in place in the home they love or assisting them to improve their financial well-being, HomeEquity Bank is here for our customers—and that's only becoming even more so as each year passes.

So, how did we get here? Let's take a walk down memory lane and see how we've grown into the organization we are today.

We've come a long way! HomeEquity Bank logos through the years.

HomeEquity Bank originated in 1986 with the launch of the Canadian Home Income Plan (CHIP), now better known by the name of our flagship product, the CHIP Reverse Mortgage. The company first came on my radar personally when I was working for the investment arm of a large bank. William Turner, founder of CHIP, had asked to meet with me to talk business. Turns out, even I was misinformed about reverse mortgages at that time! But after an hour-and-a-half conversation with William, I was convinced that CHIP was an amazing, unique product.

From a business perspective, I also saw incredible potential, considering how few banks were then focused on serving the 55-plus demographic. Beyond business, it struck me that this company offered a way that I could make a difference for an underserved demographic that needed it, and do some good for older Canadians at the same time. Within a few years of meeting William Turner, I joined the organization. I started as Chief Financial Officer in 1997. Then I was appointed president in 1998 and CEO in 2001.

When I first got here, we weren't even a bank and we were only operating in two provinces (Ontario and British Columbia). So that was my first goal: to expand our reach across Canada. Job number one was to get licensed in every province, since we wanted to become a national firm. For banks that were already operating across the country, being national ourselves meant that they could refer clients to us in every province. We started with Alberta and then grew from there. In many places where we established a presence, customers had been waiting a long time for the option of a reverse mortgage to become available.

Over the years, we expanded tremendously. In 2002, I led HomeEquity Bank through the public offering of Home Equity Income Trust that led us to become a public company listed on the Toronto Stock Exchange. In October 2009, we became a Schedule I Canadian bank, governed by the Canada Bank Act. As a bank, we are regulated by the Office of the Superintendent of Financial Institutions (OSFI), and we are a member of the Canadian Bankers Association.

We know it is important to our clients to work with a reputable organization. After all, when it comes to reverse mortgages, it often means dealing with people's most valuable asset. It's crucial that they make an informed decision and deal with a trusted organization. HomeEquity has been in business for more than 34 years. We are a federally regulated financial institution with tremendous endorsements from CARP and the Royal Canadian Legion, and we've received hundreds of positive reviews on the independent site www.trustpilot.com, some of which are featured throughout the book.

In addition to our established reputation, we are also concerned that every client feels they have done their due diligence for themselves. That's why we ask every customer to meet with an independent lawyer before they sign their reverse mortgage documents with HomeEquity Bank. Why do we do that? We believe in transparency. When it comes to signing mortgage documents later in life, we want to make sure our clients are protected from any undue influence. Should any issues arrive years down the road, we want to make sure that not just our bank, but also our customer, is protected.

Over the past few years, we've been recognized repeatedly as one of Canada's fastest-growing companies. We've been named to *Canadian Business* magazine's Growth 500 list for five years in a row. We were also included in the inaugural *Globe and Mail* Report on Business list of Canada's Top Growing Companies in 2019.

Yvonne Ziomecki and Steven Ranson celebrate HomeEquity
Bank being named to the inaugural *Globe and Mail*'s Report on
Business list of Canada's Top Growing Companies in 2019.

While staying true to our focus on reverse mortgages, we've
improved our offerings over the years. We made reverse mortgages
more flexible, expanding our products to reflect the changing needs
of older Canadians. In 2013, we added **Income Advantage** to our
lineup, which allows customers to take out their money monthly,
instead of all at once in a lump sum, improving their regular cash
flow. In 2019, we launched a product called **CHIP Max,** for clients

who are looking to get the maximum available mortgage amount. This is a great product for customers who may want to pay out debt, pay off a conventional mortgage, and more.

Customer input is very important to us. As a result of customer research and market need, we added a new product in fall 2020 called **CHIP Open**. It allows people to use our product for a shorter term than the traditional CHIP product. Plus, we are offering CHIP Open to clients with a slightly higher interest rate but no pre-payment penalties, which offers great flexibility during uncertain times such as a pandemic.

We're always trying to think of new things that would benefit our clients, while at the same time staying the course with our flagship CHIP Reverse Mortgage product that is our core expertise. We've grown our portfolio from $100 million when I joined in 1997, to more than $4 billion today. In 2020, we originated $833 million in new reverse mortgages—a number that signals how much Canadians trust our products and are finding a better lifestyle because of them. Over the years, HomeEquity Bank has helped tens of thousands of Canadians retire in the homes they love.

We've also raised our profile as a national company. While there still may be some myths and misunderstandings about the reverse mortgage, more and more people recognize CHIP and the HomeEquity Bank brand. Increasingly, people are seeing what we offer as an option that might work for them. We continue to educate Canadians about reverse mortgages and other options they may have in retirement, such as downsizing, renting, lines of credit and others. While no solution is perfect for everyone, we find that more and more people are considering CHIP as part of their retirement plan. Some use it to pay off other debt, others to improve their cash flow and standard of living, others to go on holidays, others to help their families, and others to renovate their homes or pursue personal passions. The choice is entirely theirs.

But regardless of how our customers use the money, one thing is constant: they all love their homes and want to stay living there as long as possible. Did you know that 93 percent of Canadians aged 65 and up want to stay in their current home during retirement? We've done our own surveys that confirm this desire time and time again. And our products help them do just that. Our homes are full of memories, providing not only shelter but also emotional refuge. Selling up and moving out is not just a financial decision for many people. Our homes are everything, and I think that's been even more true during the COVID-19 pandemic.

President and CEO Steven Ranson celebrates 20 years at HomeEquity Bank—with cake!

Personally, I love my home. My wife and I bought our first house when we had been married just a year, after we had saved and even borrowed from my father-in-law. The house where we live now is my third home, and they've all been in the same neighbourhood, which I also love—enough to have spent the last 37 years here! We moved into our current house in 1994, and I liked it the moment I first walked in: the physical space, the size and the fact that it's on a corner lot, so it gets great light. We even have a sunroom off the back where I have a nice desk when I need to work from home. It's a comforting space to come home to, and I like spending time there.

That's something I know I share in common with my clients, this pride in our homes and the life we've built there. I believe that this love of home is only going to grow in the future. The past year has given us even more reasons to appreciate where we live, with a global pandemic that forced us to slow down and live life more at home. For all of us, and especially the older generation, watching the tragedy unfold in long-term care homes has created even more reason to find new ways to age in place as well as advocate for change in that system.

I would like to introduce you to Yvonne Ziomecki, who heads up the Consumer Division at HomeEquity Bank and has been a member of my executive team since 2013. Yvonne is a passionate marketer, and under her leadership we have continued to expand through our television and online advertising, improving our products and listening to customers. Yvonne appears frequently on TV as an aging expert, and in 2020 she co-hosted the *Retirement Life Show*—a weekly radio show on Toronto's AM640. Yvonne is very passionate about our customers. She talks with them frequently and really understands their needs. You'll learn more about Yvonne, in her own words, in the Introduction that follows and in the personal stories she shares throughout the book.

By reading this book, you will get a chance to get to know our products as well as retirement trends, interesting home improvement options and much more. I hope the information you find here will provide you not only with a clear and useful explanation of our reverse mortgage product, but also give you inspiration through reading the stories of our clients and colleagues.

INTRODUCTION

Yvonne Ziomecki stands in front of her current home in Toronto.

I bought my first house when I was 30 years old. I had just become a new mom. It was a huge life event for me, as it is for many people.

It had been 11 years since I arrived in Canada. Ever since immigrating to this country from Poland at age 19, purchasing my own home was near the top of my goals list. In my first years here, I'd already checked off some major milestones: I'd improved my English-speaking skills, I'd completed my undergraduate degree, I'd established my career, and now I'd started a family. After my daughter Sophie was born, I felt the time was right. Owning my own home would be the next step in my "adulting," as today's young people call it. I wasn't in a hurry, but I was looking around.

Like many aspiring homeowners, I often found myself strolling around the areas where I was interested in buying a property. For me, that was Leslie and Sheppard in Toronto. The new TTC subway line was not yet built then, but I liked how walkable the neighbourhood was and how inviting the streets seemed. As I pushed Sophie along in her carriage, I'd look in to houses, as one does, judging the decor through the windows, dreaming of which one could be mine. Then one day, I saw it: my first house. The one that would actually become my first home.

The first time I viewed the interior of the house was at an estate sale. It turned out that the owner was a Finnish man who had lived alone and passed away. Now his friends were selling the contents. I found nothing useful there, but by the end of the summer a sign appeared on the lawn, advertising the house for private sale. I jotted down the phone number and made the call.

If you think this story is leading to the discovery of a hidden gem, believe me, it wasn't. This house had an ugly brown linoleum floor and sparkly orange countertops in the single bathroom. The bedrooms were small, and the owner had been a smoker. Not attractive features. But there were good bones: a big basement that I knew I could renovate into a family room, and a decent-sized backyard with a nice garden and fruit trees, overlooking a park. It felt like a good starter home.

So, like all first-time home buyers, I found myself in the whirlwind of all the tasks I needed to complete in order to buy it. In my case, the seller was the man's daughter, who lived in Finland, adding an extra layer of complexity. I gathered up the money, found a lawyer, presented the offer, and it was accepted.

WHAT'S YOUR STORY?

Working for HomeEquity Bank, I am always listening to stories about home ownership. All the paths are different. Some people are still in the house they thought would be their starter home, decades later, too in love with it to leave. Some traded up, to accommodate a growing family or to reduce their commute for a new job or to try out a quieter suburb after living in the bustling city.

Another common factor in home-purchasing decisions is that they are ultimately driven by life itself. Getting married, having a baby or just pursuing adulting—for many, the decision to buy a home has much to do with finding a sense of place in the world. And in retrospect, many also consider it the best financial decision they've ever made, especially given the real estate market in recent years. Whatever the home or circumstance, there's always a story.

Where the stories converge is in the fact that as we get older, we all want to stay in our homes. Whether it's a bungalow in Nova Scotia, a condo in downtown Calgary or a townhouse in British

Columbia, it's our houses that hold the memories and stories of our lives. Our homes are the places where we've seen our kids take their first steps and where we've spent many a morning with a coffee or tea in the back garden or on the balcony. They're where we've celebrated happy occasions and sought refuge during trying times. And now, in the midst of a global pandemic, they've become our safe havens.

Besides hearing anecdotally that most people want to "age in place," we've read study after study confirming that a vast majority of seniors would like to stay in their home as they get older. One of the latest to confirm this was a March 2020 report titled *2020 Generational Real Estate Trends Report: Aging in Place* by Mustel Group and Sotheby's International Realty Canada, which reported that 86 percent of baby boomers/older adult home-owners in Canada's key metropolitan areas want to live in their current home for as long as possible. Our own HomeEquity Bank surveys regularly confirm that over 90 percent of Canadians would like to age in place.

In this book, you'll read lots of stories about our customers and their love of place. For example, Susan Stewart, whose profile is featured in a later chapter. She lives in a condo in Coquitlam, BC, where she enjoys just the right mix of city bustle and quiet. Or the Chung family near Montreal, Quebec, who were looking for a solution to some debt problems and found it in our reverse mortgage product. Or Angelo Abbate from Ajax, Ontario, who was working into his seventies and found more balance in his life with a reverse mortgage that allows him and his wife to live more comfortably. You'll also hear from some of our amazing colleagues at HomeEquity Bank, the people who help take care of our clients from the front lines of our business. They share some great stories about their favourite clients! You'll definitely see why it's so rewarding to work here.

We've also asked some expert voices to help us pack this book with information. We'll be checking in with a lawyer whose practice focuses on older adults; an esteemed economics professor from the University of British Columbia; and even one of our favourite contractors, who specializes in accessible home renovations.

Perhaps our most special guest is one of Canada's foremost experts on aging, Dr. Samir Sinha. Dr. Sinha is Director of Health Research for Ryerson University's National Institute on Ageing, as well as Director of Geriatrics at Mount Sinai and the University Health Network hospitals in Toronto. You may recognize Dr. Sinha from his multiple appearances on television and radio providing expert counsel during the pandemic, so we're delighted that he's also taken the time to provide his advice on topics from government policy to how to age like a silver fox.

A big thanks to all of our contributors for making this book an even stronger resource!

MEET THE TEAM BEHIND HOMEEQUITY BANK

The HomeEquity Bank team rallies for a Habitat for Humanity build in Mississauga (2019).

Despite being in business since 1986 and growing in leaps and bounds both in terms of size and reputation, our culture here feels much younger, almost like a start-up. We're flexible and nimble. We're dedicated users of technology. We do a lot of videoconferencing. Unlike most banks, we don't have branches. Instead, we work with people over the phone and online. We have an office in midtown Toronto, but many of our employees work remotely. We were working from home before it was necessary during the pandemic.

While the company employs almost 250 people, it feels both big and small at the same time. Our culture is very close-knit, with a strong emphasis on open communication. We have company-wide monthly meetings to check in on each other and talk about our clients. Sometimes people cry at these meetings, over a touching story about a client whose life we've helped improve. We're really a "people business" in every way.

But we don't expect you just to take our word for it. And so, we'd like to introduce you to some of our people, who are just as dedicated to

HomeEquity Bank as we are. You'll find several "Meet the Team" Q&As sprinkled throughout this book. Every one of our employees shares an ambition to help older people live their best lives. In fact, a number of our employees have even brought their parents and family members on as clients! They were also very eager to help when we asked them to share stories of their favourite clients. We hope you will enjoy hearing from them.

MEET THE TEAM: CLIVE COKE, REGIONAL VICE PRESIDENT

What's your background?

I've been at HomeEquity Bank since 2015, after several years at other banks in different mortgage and sales roles. I lead a sales team of about nine business development managers. Because what we offer customers is so different than what's out there in the market-place, much of what we do is educate. We spend a lot of time with mortgage brokers.

Who stands out as a memorable client?

My favourite client story is my very first client. She's a widow who was around 70 years old when I met her. Her husband had recently passed away. With his death came a loss of income to her household. So, she found herself in a position where she wasn't able financially to maintain the house on her own. And she actually ended up in the collections department of her bank. But then someone at the bank remembered that HomeEquity Bank could potentially help her.

So, we met with her and reviewed her situation. And not only were we able to help her, we were able to put her in a position where she would also have additional money to help her children. And we still stay in touch, even today! We'll grab breakfast once in a blue moon and call each other over the holidays just to say hi. We just share a special con-nection. And she's doing great. I think she appreciates the fact that we stay connected.

> **What do you like about working for HomeEquity Bank?**
>
> I have an awesome, amazing team. We're really committed not only to growing individually as employees, but also as a group. That's a powerful thing when you get the synergy of all of that coming together. The other thing I really enjoy is the culture. We spend a lot of time making a culture that's open, accessible, that's willing to hear a different way of thinking and different opinions. We're an organization that is very open to new ideas.

WAYS WE CONNECT WITH OUR CUSTOMERS

Statistics Canada notes that as of July 2020, there were over 6.8 million Canadians over the age of 65. At HomeEquity Bank, our customer base is even broader—Canadians over the age of 55—and we do a lot to understand and to connect them. In addition to personally speaking with our clients, we regularly commission market research to find out more about them, from what they understand about our product to what communications platforms they like best.

Time and time again, they return results that are not terribly surprising: Most older people don't think of themselves as old. They see themselves as being empowered, in control and very much able. Market research also reveals that most older Canadians hate the stereotypical advertising out there that depicts older people as either frail and feeble or as silly caricatures in ads for sex enhancement commercials.

At HomeEquity Bank, we also pay attention to the ways that our customers connect with us. Many find out about HomeEquity Bank by watching our TV commercials. You may have seen some of them over the years, too, with our iconic yellow bar at the bottom. Some of our ads are animated, and some feature real customers telling their personal stories. In recent years, some have been a bit cheeky, poking fun at the senior stereotypes that irritate us all. Some simply explain the product and ask people to call for a no-obligation quote.

For a number of years, some of our favourite ads have featured the famous Canadian figure skater Kurt Browning, who is an ambassador for our product. He really believes in reverse mortgages and the power they have to change customers' lives.

Canadian figure skater and HomeEquity Bank Ambassador Kurt Browning in a HomeEquity Bank commercial.

In recent years, we've found that more and more people like to go online and learn about CHIP Reverse Mortgages in their own time. Our website www.chip.ca is packed with information. You'll also find a Question-and-Answer section, blog posts and customer reviews. Our website evolves based on what our customers want to read about and how they want to read the information. My favourite section of the website is the one with calculators—that's where you can find out how much money you qualify for simply by answering a few questions! You can also figure out how much your house will be worth down the road and how much equity you will have left. Pretty powerful tools.

Over the past few years, both Steven Ranson, our president and CEO, and I have been very active in the media. We frequently appear on TV across the country, speaking about our company, our products and our customers. You may have seen Steven on BNN Bloomberg—he also gets interviewed by major newspapers across the country. I have been active on TV, touring the country from coast to coast as an aging expert and talking to people about how reverse mortgages can help many Canadians age in place.

In my appearances on CTV, Global, CHCH and other outlets, I discuss a range of subjects, from serious to fun, educating Canadians on topics such as protecting our loved ones from fraud, improving our homes with accessible renovations, and using fun gadgets. I've even demonstrated adaptive clothing that helps to ensure everyone can age in style. I have also co-hosted a weekly *Retirement Life Show* on AM640 with the über-talented

John Scholes. We have covered pretty much every financial aspect of retirement on our show.

Yvonne Ziomecki with John Scholes, co-hosting the
***Retirement Life Show* on Toronto's AM640.**

And, of course, this book is one of the latest ways Steven and I have come up with to reach out to our customers. We wanted to find a way to both share the stories of our inspiring clients as well as to provide a guide to the reverse mortgage that debunks some of the myths out there. These myths prevent people who could really use this product from seeing its benefits, and I'm determined to educate as many people as I can. I want to help them understand how it truly works so they can truly consider it as an option.

HOW TO READ THIS BOOK

We'd love for you to read this book straight through, as we've created each section to build on the next, painting a picture of the real estate market in Canada and how it connects with the reverse mortgage product. We've also taken the time to collect client stories both directly and through our friendly staff. They're sprinkled throughout the book. But we know that you're all busy people, so if you've in a hurry, feel free to just flip straight to the chapters most relevant to you.

In Chapter One, we look at the perfect storm that's made reverse mortgages a great option for Canadians: the fantastic real estate market on the total upside coupled with the decline in pensions and other financial challenges facing aging Canadians. This chapter also features our first contribution from geriatrician Dr. Samir Sinha, reflecting on some of the systemic problems in our senior care system.

Chapter Two addresses all you ever wanted to know about reverse mortgages: how they work, frequently asked questions, and examples of how people use them. We also discuss some of HomeEquity Bank's other products, including **Income Advantage** (which lets you borrow on a regular basis rather than a lump sum) and **CHIP Max** (which allows more borrowing than our standard product). We also look at **CHIP Open**, our latest product (which offers the most flexibility for clients who want to repay their reverse mortgage early due to changing circumstances).

Chapter Three takes a closer look at "the new retiree"—the real person whose multi-dimensionality transcends all the stereotypes we've learned about old age. In Chapter Four, we look at what's needed for this remarkable senior to age in place, welcoming more of Dr. Sinha's advice on how to age like a silver fox. Chapter Five tackles some of the alternatives to reverse mortgages, from downsizing to lines of credit. In Chapter Six, we provide some tips on how to talk about finances with your family. We also consider some of the professionals you might want to speak to as you explore the reverse mortgage product.

Chapter Seven looks at tools that will help you to stay in the home you love, and shares some tips to help you audit your house for safety risks as you get older. We've also included gadgets and tips to help you deal with some of the tiresome downsides of old age, from smart appliances that shut off automatically to gardening seats that offer relief for your tired back.

In Chapter Eight, we reflect on ageism and how we can do better to support our senior population, along with some things our government, families and friends can do. In the Afterword, HomeEquity Bank President and CEO Steven Ranson shares his ideas and hopes for the future of reverse mortgages and, indeed, the prosperity of older people into the future.

WHO SHOULD READ THIS BOOK?

While we hope that every Canadian would want to read this book, we did write it with a couple of specific audiences in mind. First and foremost, we wrote it for those who are 55 or older and who may be considering a reverse mortgage or simply want to learn more about this innovative product.

Another audience we had in mind when writing is adult children who are trying to discover new options for their aging parents. We know from experience that concerned adult children are some of the first to come across the reverse mortgage product and reach out to us with questions about its suitability for their parents. They may also find it helpful to consider a reverse mortgage for their own retirement planning down the road.

We also hope that this book might have some second readers. So, if you're finished reading this guide, consider passing it along to any Canadian over 55 who you think could benefit from learning about the reverse mortgage option. After you've read it yourself, that is. Enjoy!

CHAPTER ONE

CANADA'S UNSTOPPABLE REAL ESTATE MARKET

Welcome to the neighbourhood! Peonies from Yvonne's favourite local shop.

I wrote in the Introduction about my personal journey to home ownership, when I found the cute little house that was far from perfect but came along at just the right time for me. As I grew in it, I made it even more my own, painting the walls, changing most fixtures and buying new appliances. The biggest renovation was to the kitchen, and I remember the first time I cooked in the renovated version thinking, "This is mine!" Finally, I was truly home.

Another pleasant surprise of owning my home was finding a new community of people in my neighbourhood. At my first house, one of the most delightful encounters I had was meeting the next-door neighbours. The day we moved in, Diana and Kevin showed up with a cake. They said they were so glad to get good neighbours. Even though we're no longer neighbours (they moved to Kingston a few years ago, and I've made another couple of moves myself), I'm still in touch with them today. Their friendship is an excellent reminder that buying a home isn't just about bricks and mortar: it's about the relationships and the new journeys you go on with others in your neighbourhood.

My two daughters and I love our current house and our Toronto neighbourhood! Probably more than any we've lived in before, because we use it so much. There's the corner shop where I regularly grab fresh peonies (my favourite) and the wings place where we have our regular Tuesday night family dates. I love walking in the nearby parks, and the fact that I can walk to work is a great way to prepare for and unwind from my day. When I ask my clients for their own favourite parts of their neighbourhoods, their answers are like mine. Even more so when they've lived in a neighbourhood for decades and seen it mature along with their kids.

Almost as much as our homes, our neighbourhoods are something that we give up when we move. When we downsize, it's not often that we can buy back into our same neighbourhood. And trying to find all those "favourites" again, whether it's a doctor or a coffee shop, is hard, especially when we're older. To me, this is one of the best arguments in favour of our reverse mortgage product. That you not only don't need to give up your home, but you don't need to leave your neighbourhood either. For most Canadians, buying a home and buying into the neighbourhood that we've grown to love, has been one of the best financial decisions of our lives. So, why not stay?

In this chapter, we're going to take a look at some of the factors that have emerged to create the kind of environment where the reverse mortgage can shine as a financial solution. One of these factors is very positive—the decision by so many older Canadians to buy a house and the good fortune of an unstoppable real estate market that has been rising for decades and created vast wealth for homeowners. We'll also look at the downsides of many people's current economic realities—the fact that many jobs now come with lower-quality pensions, and the fact that many Canadians have been caught off guard and not saved adequately for retirement.

When you look at this combination, you realize that many older Canadians are house-rich but looking at a retirement that may be lifestyle-poor, unless they find a way to extract some cash from their home investment. That's where the reverse mortgage product fits in as an option for more people than you'd expect. Finally, we've asked aging expert Dr. Samir Sinha to help provide a snapshot of what Canada's support system for seniors looks like in terms of both health care and finances.

CANADA'S FANTASTIC REAL ESTATE MARKET

Did we know when we bought our houses that we were making such a fantastic financial decision at the time? No. But it's been a shared goal for many Canadians for decades—in fact, a Statistics Canada survey shows that 63 percent of Canadian families own their homes as of 2016. But as we buy, we're not thinking about our peers (okay, well, maybe part of us is thinking about keeping up with those Joneses, but what's wrong with a little friendly competition?) so much as we are thinking that we need a place to live, to provide stability for our growing families.

Whether it be to celebrate the fact that we finally landed a permanent job or to establish roots in a city or town we jived with, we each have our own reasons why it was time to buy a home. Then, as we went on with our lives, paying our mortgages off bit by bit, our houses kept appreciating! Maybe we took action to build the value as well: a bathroom reno here, a back deck there, maybe even a full extension if the house suddenly seemed small.

How much did the value of our houses grow? Those who live outside Toronto joke about Torontonians believing their city is the centre of the world, but it has done pretty well in terms of housing prices. Average prices have gone from $30,426 in 1971 to $189,105 in 1987 to $566,696 in 2014. More recently, the Toronto Real Estate Board for October 2020 shows that the average sale price was $960,772—up by 14 percent year over year. The climb continues in the rest of the country as well: the Canadian Real Estate Association reported in September 2020 that the average price of a Canadian resale home was $604,000, up 17.5 percent from the average price a year earlier. You only need to ask a boomer to confirm that the investment in property, particularly when it's your own home, is extraordinarily worthwhile. Remember my starter home I purchased in 2000 for $276,000? It's probably worth $1.5 million today.

Interest rates have also dropped. Even back when I bought my first house in the early 2000s, the interest rate was around 7 percent. A client who bought her home in 1982 reports that rates were more than 19 percent in that era! By 2015, the rate had dropped to 3.8 percent, and the late 2020 rate hovered around 2 percent for a five-year mortgage.

The lowering of interest rates led to there being even more focus on the real estate market, sometimes to the point of craziness that you read about today, with bidding wars for tiny lots in Toronto or multiple offers on a teardown in Vancouver. Those of us who bought into the market when houses were priced in the high $200s during the early 2000s (or in the five figures even earlier!) shake our heads. That is, unless we've recently tried to trade up or help our kids get into the housing market. We understand how serious the battle can be for younger people.

For me, getting into the market when I did and seeing my property value rise, makes me quite reluctant to sell my property anytime soon. Because of the spectacular growth over recent decades, I think even those who bought a house more recently and have experienced the opportunity to see it grow would agree with me. My millennial friends who bought condos or houses five or 10 years ago have seen remarkable growth, too. Moreover, owning a home is, of course, more than an investment. For me, it's where I've raised my two girls, Sophie and Helen, experienced some of life's ups and downs, hosted amazing friends and created lifelong memories.

THE UNFORTUNATE DEBT LOAD OF OLDER CANADIANS

While the windfall that is the housing market to date is definitely an upside for older Canadians, many face some financial obstacles. Statistics show that older people carry more debt today than ever before. According to Statistics Canada, the proportion of senior families with debt was 42 percent in 2016, up from 27 percent in 1999. The median amount of debt was $25,000 in 2016, up from $9,000 in 1999 (expressed in 2016 constant dollars). The share of those with consumer debt increased from 24 percent to 37 percent.

On the upside, the median level of assets held by senior families in 2016 also rose, from $327,000 to $607,400 (in 2016 constant dollars). Many Canadians may be carrying mortgages, but they also have assets worth more than the debt. In 2016, the median net worth (assets minus debt) of senior families with debt was $537,400, up from $298,900 in 1999.

But Canadians are also looking for ways to improve their finances. According to the 2016 census report on income statistics for senior families 65 and over, of 5.3 million senior households, the median income (where half are lower and half are higher) was

$27,353 and the average income was $40,862. In a 2018 report titled *Reasons for Working at 60 and Beyond*, Statistics Canada noted that according to the Labour Force Survey, workers in 2017 were retiring on average at 64 years of age, almost three years later than in the late 1990s. Coinciding with an increase in retirement age, the last 20 years have seen a near doubling of the labour force participation rate for those aged 60 years and over, from 14 percent in 1997 to 26 percent in 2017.

If these numbers suggest that many people you know may be working longer or carrying more debt than you realize (it's not just you!), we can verify that as well. Most people who need the bit of extra help that the reverse mortgage provides don't show their debt outwardly: they're not wearing tattered clothing or avoiding every social gathering. But we've also met couples who had not enjoyed a bottle of wine at home on a Saturday night in three years. Or other couples who quit socializing regularly with their neighbours. In each situation, they coped silently with the pinch of their debt and didn't want to say a word.

Another challenge was the great recession of 2008, when many boomers found their portfolios hit hard at exactly the time of life when they were more vulnerable to such a loss, without a great window of time before retirement to recover. The *Reasons for Working at 60 and Beyond* report argues that the 2008–09 recession and the related global financial crisis, combined with the decline in pension coverage and the shift from defined-benefit to defined-contribution pension plans in the 1990s and 2000s, may have made it harder for a portion of this population to accumulate sufficient savings and wealth for retirement. The National Institute on Ageing's *National Seniors Strategy* (Third Edition) notes that similar losses would be felt by older Canadians who sold off their investments at the start of the pandemic in March 2020.

So, while house prices were still climbing, the remainder of retirement-ready boomers' portfolios were facing new uncertainties. And it's not just older folks feeling the burden of debt. In June 2020, Statistics Canada reported that Canada's debt-to-income ratio (the measure of how much debt a household is carrying) relative to its disposable income, was almost 177 percent, meaning that for every dollar a Canadian had to spend, they owed $1.77.

We have all experienced setbacks in our lives and we all know, both in our own lives and from hearing about others' lives, that it's not always the case that everything constantly gets better and better or magically falls into place. Sometimes people get into debt and struggle to pay it off. Bringing clients, who have long thought that they would just have to accept being under constant stress, into the realization that they could use their home as an asset—the one they were smart enough to invest in years ago—is our favourite way of helping our clients. We love to see that look of relief on their faces!

Reflecting on the debt burden of older Canadians is a good reminder of a story from a few years back, about a couple from BC. Mary was 75 and John was 87 when we met them. John had gotten sick and the couple was living off his pensions, thinking it was enough for life. Retirement and old age had once seemed far away, but then Mary said that "one day down the road" just "showed up." She had regret but also shared that she felt regret was a useless emotion. When she signed up for the CHIP Reverse Mortgage, she saw it as a second chance. She thanked us profusely for helping to get a grip on their finances. She said she slept like a baby the night she finally signed for the reverse mortgage. She told us she felt like she had been drowning and we pulled her out of hot water. Hearing the depth of gratitude she expressed was such a thrill for us as a company!

"They gave me peace of mind when I was stressed out for what the future held. They gave me the means to be able to stay in my own home for the foreseeable future."
- D. Pierson

Rated on Trustpilot   HomeEquity Bank

DECLINE IN PENSIONS

In addition to being in debt, a 2017 Statistics Canada report showed that only 37 percent of paid workers were covered by a registered pension plan. Add to that the decline in deluxe "defined-benefit" type pension plans that were the gold standard for Canadians in years past. Defined-benefit plans are the kind where the money an employee receives in retirement is fixed and based on a formula. For example, if an employee earns $50,000 in their last five years of work and they worked for 30 years and they get 2 percent of that salary, then their total pension is fixed at $50,000 x 30 years x 2 percent = $30,000 annually. The employer has committed to providing that amount regardless of how the organization's investments fare. However, the joint Healthcare of Ontario Pension Plan/National Institute on Ageing report *The Value of a Good Pension: How to Improve the Efficiency of Retirement Savings in Canada* notes that only 10 percent of private sector workers are covered by defined-benefit pensions—about a third of the coverage of the late 1970s.

By contrast, "defined-contribution" pension plans require that both employer and employee contribute, but the money received in retirement is not guaranteed by the employer, so both are taking the risk on the investments. Putting money into a defined-contribution plan is still smart because employers often match employee contributions, but the defined-benefit model is more secure.

You probably don't need to think very long to come up with someone you know who has no pension at all. Or scarier, no savings. The *Value of a Good Pension* report argues that Canadians need the help of official pension programs, as they result in $5.32 compared with $1.70 using a typical individual approach. Furthermore, a 2016 study by the Broadbent Institute showed that the median value of retirement assets of Canadians aged 45 to 64 is only just over $3,000.

More recently, a CIBC poll from 2018 showed that 30 percent of Canadians have no retirement savings and 19 percent have saved less than $50,000. Add to all this, the positive news: Canadians are living longer than ever before. The life expectancy of Canadians aged 55 is 80 for men and 84 for women, and that's a lot longer to plan for living in retirement (for a woman retiring at 65, it's nearly 20 years!). But the average Canada Pension Plan payout for March 2020 was just under $700, which most people need to supplement in order to have a decent standard of living.

For some people, their life's work was found in a field where pensions weren't standard. Or maybe they ran their own business. Or maybe they worked for one of the many companies that only hire on contract, no longer offering such luxuries as pensions. Or maybe they belong to a more at-risk category. The National Institute on Ageing's January 2016 report *An Evidence-Informed National Seniors Strategy for Canada*, Second Edition, highlights that single, unattached older adults as well as older women remain the most financially vulnerable population, partly due to a greater likelihood of gaps in their workforce participation, combined with longer life expectancy. The report also argues that current retirement savings vehicles and public pension plan programs are falling short in supporting older Canadians.

The bottom line is that pensions are becoming a less reliable source of income for retirees in Canada, and we haven't figured out how much we should be saving. We're not always the best at planning for retirement when we see it as "down the road." But we did make that one good decision in purchasing a house—so why not unlock some of the savings inside it?

THIS CHANGES EVERYTHING:
COVID-19 AND THE LONG-TERM-CARE FIASCO

As of March 2020, it is no longer possible to write anything about the state of our country, economy or society without mentioning the huge impact of the global pandemic. At the time when we were writing this book last summer and fall, Canadians were starting to grapple with the longevity of COVID-19 and the changes the virus brought to our society. We roll with the punches as easygoing Canadians, but this was an unprecedented time—in fact, it's possible that the word "unprecedented" has never been used as much as it was in those early days when everything seemed so uncertain.

People became furloughed or unemployed, and the news was full of sadness and dark uncertainty, first from places overseas like Wuhan, China, and then Italy and Spain. Then the news got closer with case numbers in Canada on the rise, and it felt patriotic to make certain sacrifices like our extended lockdowns. As our cases began to drop in the summer while we watched with worry as the US pandemic numbers soared. In the fall, children returned to school, bars and restaurants opened for business and then closed again, as the number of new cases started to rise. And the story goes on—we don't need to tell you, you've lived it.

All in all, it's been a once-in-a-lifetime shift, sure to permanently change everything from the way we congregate and socialize to the way we earn a living and look at our houses. Hopefully there will be some positive consequences long-term, like the mainstreaming of technologies we never used much (hello, videoconferencing), and there certainly have been some profound acts of human kindness and giving that are very inspiring. But it is also a time for reflection on what we hold dear.

In Canada, a collective sadness was felt for those in our long-term care facilities who were the hardest hit in the early phase of COVID-19 here. When a Canadian Institute for Health Information (CIHI) report in late May 2020 showed that over 80 percent of COVID-19 deaths in Canada occurred in long-term care facilities, we learned as a country that we need to do better for our seniors. In fact, it also showed that the number of deaths in Canada's long-term care facilities were nearly double the average of other countries in the Organization for Economic Co-operation and Development (OECD). The report furthermore noted that outbreaks were recorded in 840 nursing and retirement facilities as of late May, with over five thousand deaths. It was a clear wake-up call to do more for these citizens; one that had politicians promising to call inquires and work on better regulations and eventually promise improved funding.

While the tragedy in long-term care homes provides yet another argument for the benefits of aging in place as long as possible, we are not arguing at all that society should turn its head away from this unfortunate situation. While some may be able to put supports in place to stay in their homes for longer, we still need to work to improve this system that should be a safety net for anyone who needs it.

Because even before the pandemic, health care affordability was a problem. CIHI projected that health spending in Canada would reach over $264 billion in 2019 and represent 11.6 percent of Canada's gross domestic product, equal to $7,068 per Canadian. The Fraser Institute's *The Price of Public Health Care Insurance, 2020* report suggests that the average payment for insurance ranges from $4,190 to $14,474. We know from our own bills that this can include such costs as prescription drugs, mobility aids, dental care, physiotherapy, hearing aids and glasses.

And as the baby boomer generation continues to age, these problems may grow worse. A 2019 Ipsos survey commissioned by the Canadian Medical Association showed that 88 percent of Canadians are worried about the costs our aging population poses to the health care system and that 58 percent believe that Canadians will have to delay their retirement to afford their health care. The cost of hiring private health care support is expensive, as home support and personal care costs between $20 and $30 per hour, with professional services like nursing and therapy costing between $50 and $60 a visit, depending on the service. Moving to a retirement home is another option, but it can cost more than $5,000 per month.

A LOVE OF HOME AND PLACE

One hopeful upside to emerge from the pandemic was the reinforcement of our love of home. While not being able to venture far beyond my neighbourhood or see my friends or go to concerts, the pandemic did make me really cherish the fact that I have a safe and comfortable place to live. And most importantly, my girls were with me. My eldest daughter, Sophie, who had been at university, moved back in. And Helen, my younger daughter, attended online classes from her bedroom.

As Steven mentioned in his Foreword, when the pandemic hit, as a bank, we spent some time calling clients to check in, an initiative we called Operation Warm Hug. Many clients echoed our sentiments, expressing profound sadness over the worldwide changes but also some joy in the fact that they had a place where they felt safe to cloister for however long the turmoil continued.

HomeEquity Bank President and CEO Steven Ranson at his home, calling clients for Operation Warm Hug.

Like me, our clients see their home not only as their address but also their sanctuary. Often it was their first big adult purchase. The place where they became a real couple and where they saw their kids achieve milestones from first steps to first birthdays to first bike rides along the sidewalk out front. It's a place that holds too many sweet memories to abandon easily. And frankly, to return to the upside that we highlighted earlier in the chapter, there's too much value in a home to give it up these days. We mentioned above how much the average home value is increasing, but beyond those numbers, we hear every day about the ways that individuals' homes have gone up in value. Imagine the fact that some people bought their homes in the 1970s for five figures—unheard of these days!

So, each of our customers not only has this incredible investment, but also a nest egg growing inside it. Granted, there are some who say that the best way to hatch this nest egg is to sell and redeem the cash value inside it, but that's an idea that's easier said than done from the examples we've seen. Consider the expenses involved with moving: the cost of realtor fees being one enormous expense. Five percent on the October 2020 average Toronto home price of $960,772 equals more than $48,000 in realtor fees. Then add a few thousand more for lawyer fees, plus the cost of moving and likely the need for new furniture at the new home. In the end, a homeowner might have to subtract over $50,000 from that sale price. (We'll look more at downsizing in Chapter Five, where we examine alternatives to the reverse mortgage.)

OPENING MINDS WITH FACTS

When people meet us, they assume we're going to try and sell them on a CHIP Reverse Mortgage immediately. That's not the case. In fact, we're always telling people that a reverse mortgage may not be for everyone. We see our role as that of helping to educate people about the reverse mortgage so they see it as another option, another retirement tool—especially if they made the fantastic decision of investing in a house earlier in their life.

In the next chapter, we're going to focus directly on the reverse mortgage itself. We'll also continue to feature anecdotes from clients and from our colleagues on the front lines of our business who share their stories of favourite clients. With their hard work, HomeEquity Bank has already helped more than sixty thousand clients accomplish everything from paying off debt, to completing long-planned renovations, to adding the ramps that allowed them to stay in their house even after a decline in mobility. We're proud that we've helped customers through the rough patches that life brings, and now we're even prouder to share their stories.

EXPERT SPOTLIGHT: DR. SAMIR SINHA ON CANADA'S AGING POPULATION

We are so excited to include the voice of leading geriatrician Dr. Samir Sinha in this book! His progressive understanding of aging respects the well-being of the entire person. While the pandemic has raised his public profile, as he's generously given much of his time to share his public health wisdom, we wanted to provide some of his bio so that you can appreciate his excellent, expert credentials.

Dr. Samir Sinha

Dr. Samir Sinha is Director of Health Research for Ryerson University's National Institute on Ageing, as well as Director of Geriatrics at Mount Sinai and the University Health Network hospitals in Toronto. In 2012, he served as the Government of Ontario's expert lead for its Seniors Strategy. Dr. Sinha is now part of a growing group of health care professionals, economists and national associations calling for a National Seniors Strategy that would address everything from housing to wellness to caregiver support.

What does our current support system for seniors look like in Canada?

Until 1900, life expectancy in Canada was only 51 years of age! Even by the time we created medicare 50 years ago, the average Canadian was only 27 years of age and most of us didn't live beyond our sixties. It wasn't until a few years ago that we started seeing older Canadians outnumbering younger Canadians for the first time in our history. In the past, most of us would work, we'd retire and be dead within a few years.

When we founded medicare, we felt that the most important things that we wanted covered at the time were physician services and hospital services. We didn't enshrine long-term care into our Canada Health Act in the 1980s. That was our original sin, to never include the provision of long-term care in our system that the federal and provincial governments support. We don't have national standards. Or quality measures. The majority of what we spend in health care is on the minority of the population who don't have access to the right models of care and supports they need. Add to that the fact that health and social care providers have not been well-trained and educated to work with older adults, and it's a problem.

What about long-term care?

We're underfunding our home care and our long-term care system by about 30 percent because it's largely sitting on the backs of the provinces to figure out how they're going to actually fund all of this care. When you have an underfunded system, and you have older, outdated facilities and trouble recruiting and retaining staff, that's what the system looked like before COVID-19 hit.

COVID-19 has exposed the level of systemic vulnerabilities that were existing, with staffers so poorly paid they're working in multiple homes to try and make ends meet. It was a perfect recipe for allowing COVID to gain a foothold in these home-care settings and then spread like wildfire. That's why Canada has that dubious distinction, out of the OECD countries, of having the highest proportion of COVID deaths happening in long-term care homes.

How does Canada's approach compare with other countries?

Did you know that in Denmark, they actually have a public health nurse come by your house and check in with you at age 75, the same way that public health nurses check on new parents in Canada when their babies are born? The Denmark nurses educate people on the kinds of things that might change due to age, and they orient citizens to supports available in their community and how to access them.

Countries like Germany, South Korea, Japan and others have also developed what they call long-term care insurance systems, where people after a certain age, maybe in their forties, for example, start paying an additional payroll tax. You pay into it, and it grows in a pot so that when you turn 65, if you actually ever do need long-term care, then you know that it will be sufficiently funded. Australia basically has an annual cap on what you would spend, so you wouldn't be expected to contribute over that, and also a lifetime cap on long-term care expenses, based on your income, not your assets.

Why do you think we're behind on this issue in Canada?

Perhaps we've always been a young country, that's relied on immigration and other factors to grow our population. When you go to countries in Europe, for example, they've always had a more sizable older population. So, they seem to have picked up on these issues a lot earlier and dealt with them more proactively. North American society is also far more ageist. We pride ourselves in being a highly youthful society, and the anti-aging industry is a massive, multi-billion-dollar business. Whereas in Asia and Europe, we see a greater appreciation for the older population and also for meeting their needs in a humanistic and appropriate way.

Most Canadians don't realize that we don't have a robust, functioning long-term care system. Unlike hospital care, which isn't rationed per se, we really have significant rationing of the limited long-term care resources we have. We have wait-lists. We have shortages of home-care services. This means that the only way people can often stay independent is if they buy privately additional services, which start adding up.

So, how do we start to take action?

We need to think about ways to reorganize our health and social care systems to recognize that more older people want to age in their homes and communities. We have a system that still prioritizes funding the institutionalization of seniors and hospitals, and nursing and retirement homes. Did you know that 87 percent of our long-term care spending is actually spent on institutionalizing people in nursing homes, as opposed to supporting them to remain in their own homes and communities? By comparison, a country like Denmark spends two-thirds of its money devoted to senior care on trying to support older people to stay in their own homes and communities.

So, Canada's in this weird situation where we spend a third less than other countries on long-term care as a percentage of our GDP. We spend 30 percent less, and the majority of that [is spent on] institutionalizing people, which is far more expensive than helping people stay healthy and independent in their own homes. This is the challenge—we've built a system that's not really aligned with what people actually want or need.

There's also a real blind spot in the fact that geriatrics is not included as much in the medical school curriculum. When older people are starting to encounter issues, who do they ask for advice? Their primary care doctors, who don't actually know all the options to help people stay healthy and independent for as long as possible.

We need to actually have a properly educated workforce, because when doctors are graduating from medical schools with no training in geriatrics, that's concerning for all of us as we age.

More on the campaign for a National Seniors Strategy: nationalseniorsstrategy.ca.

CHAPTER TWO

THE REVERSE MORTGAGE ADVANTAGE

In this chapter, we'd like to zero in on the CHIP Reverse Mortgage, the crown jewel of our business at HomeEquity Bank. In the previous chapter, we outlined the perfect storm of conditions that has really made it a great option for Canadians heading into retirement. And while we think it's an excellent product, it's sometimes frustrating that there are still so many myths and misconceptions about it.

And so, on the next pages we'll lay out the basics of the product, how to apply and what to expect during the process. We'll outline the kinds of things you might use a reverse mortgage for, we'll address some of the questions we are frequently asked and we'll also pull out some math and scenarios that show why it's a good option for many people. Maybe it's even a good option for you.

EXPERT SPOTLIGHT: DR. THOMAS DAVIDOFF

It's not just us who think the reverse mortgage is misunderstood. Dr. Thomas Davidoff, Director of the University of British Columbia's Centre for Urban Economics and Real Estate and an associate professor of Strategy and Business Economics at the University of British Columbia's Sauder School of Business, has written several articles on the topic of reverse mortgages. In 2016, puzzled by the low uptake of the reverse mortgage product, Dr. Davidoff and his colleagues, professors Patrick Gerhard and Thomas Post, conducted the first survey of US homeowners aged 58 and older to assess their knowledge about the reverse mortgage.

Published in a paper titled *Reverse Mortgages: What Homeowners (Don't) Know and How it Matters,* the study found that while awareness of reverse mortgages was high, knowledge of contract terms was limited. The study also found that those who knew more about the product and those who had peers with a reverse mortgage expressed greater intent to use them. Dr. Davidoff has said directly that part of what holds reverse mortgages back is that they're a bit complex to understand and older people don't always have the time or patience to learn about them. But by avoiding them, they are missing out on something that could hold huge benefit! So, we couldn't agree more that education is needed.

While we're going to start by explaining the reverse mortgage, probably in more detail than you've ever read before, we will also mention at the end of the chapter some of the other options that we offer at HomeEquity Bank. These are all a variation on the reverse mortgage: **Income Advantage** allows you to borrow your money at regular intervals rather than in a lump sum, which can be a great for improving cash flow. **CHIP Max** allows you to borrow more than the traditional 55 percent that we allow in a regular CHIP. And **CHIP Open** provides flexibility for early repayment without penalties. But let's get started with the basics first.

HOW A REVERSE MORTGAGE WORKS

What is a reverse mortgage? It's a loan that allows you to access the equity in your home without having to sell it. The loan is secured against the value of your home. Unlike a traditional mortgage, you don't have to make mortgage payments until the home is sold. In other countries, the reverse mortgage is sometimes called equity release.

HomeEquity Bank was founded in 1986, and originally our product was called the Canadian Home Income Plan, which was shortened to CHIP and then renamed the CHIP Reverse Mortgage. We became a Schedule I Canadian bank in 2009, and that's when we began operating as HomeEquity Bank. Our company is named HomeEquity Bank, but our flagship product is the CHIP Reverse Mortgage, so we advertise both. Sort of like the way that Toyota is the company, but Corolla is the car's name.

Here are the basic qualifications for a reverse mortgage:

- Our customers must be 55 and over and own their home.
- Everyone on the application (and home title) must be 55 and older.
- The home must be a client's primary residence.
- The home's value must be over $200,000.

Borrowers may access up to 55 percent of their home's appraised value (our CHIP Max product allows you to access more). When you apply for a reverse mortgage, HomeEquity Bank will consider your age and the age of everyone on the title of your house or living in the house; the city or area where you live; and your home's condition, type and appraised value. Generally, the older you are, the more money you may qualify for. Our average client is 72 years old and the average reverse mortgage size is $170,000.

The money you borrow is tax-free and it does not affect your Old Age Security or Guaranteed Income Supplement (GIS) benefits.

You always remain on title and retain ownership of your home. You are required to stay up-to-date on your property taxes and homeowner's insurance as well as keep your property in good condition. The CHIP Reverse Mortgage is a non-recourse loan, which means that at the time of repayment, you or your estate will never owe more than the fair market value of your home, as long as you have maintained your property, paid your property tax and have valid property insurance. This is our "No Negative Equity Guarantee."

If you want to see how much you might quality for, feel free to visit our calculators online at www.chip.ca/chip-reverse-mortgage/ and enter your details to get an estimate. If you have a mortgage on your house or lines of credit, you must pay them off when you get a reverse mortgage (i.e., roll those debts into the amount you are taking out). You can use the money from a reverse mortgage to pay any mortgage, debt or lien against your house.

Steps to securing a **Reverse Mortgage**

01 Initial phone meeting

02 Home appraisal

03 Reverse mortgage qualified amount

04 Confirm reverse mortgage loan amount & interest rate options

05 Select a lawyer to obtain independent legal advice

06 Legal process

07 Funds become available

Just like traditional mortgages, we offer interest at both fixed and variable rates and at different time spans, such as six months or five years. Unlike a regular mortgage, **you don't make regular mortgage payments on a reverse mortgage. This is the biggest benefit of our product: it allows you to stay in your home with no monthly mortgage payments.** We do have an option to make interest payments should you come into some money or want to reduce the amount of accrued interest. You can also pay off the principal and interest in full at any time; however, there are penalties for early repayment. Our new product, **CHIP Open**, provides a new option for those who expect to repay early, with no pre-payment penalties.

What many people don't realize is that when you get qualified for a reverse mortgage, you don't have to take the entire amount you are approved for. As a matter of fact, you have a lot of options. Let's use an example of a customer named Joan living in a $700,000 house in Peterborough. She gets approved for $320,000. She can:

- take the full amount of $320,000 as a lump sum at once on the date of funding,

- take a smaller amount (for example, $170,000) and forego the rest,

- take a smaller amount (for example, $170,000) but ask to have the remaining $150,000 set aside for subsequent advances, or

- take $1,000 a month for 26 years in planned advances (as an example) to supplement her income using our Income Advantage product.

APPLICATION PROCESS

The way most clients get started is by giving us a call or by visiting their bank or a mortgage broker. In our call centre we have Client Consultants on the line to answer any of your initial questions. If you have looked at our online calculators and have additional questions, we encourage you to call us or speak to one of our knowledgeable referral partners (mortgage brokers or branch staff at major Canadian banks). Talking with one of our Client Consultants is one of the best ways to get specific about your own situation. There are no obligations when you call. We will ask you a few basic questions and provide you with a quote, and we will also mail you our *CHIP Reverse Mortgage Guide*, which has a lot of information about our products. We encourage prospective clients to talk the idea over with friends and family members, anyone they trust.

The next step is to fill out an application. After we take your application, we send an independent appraiser to your home to assess its value. This cost is typically $300 to $600 and it must be covered by the homeowner. Our lawyers will do a title check on the house, and we will do a credit check. We ask for information on any existing mortgages and other debt. For most homeowners, this process will be familiar because it's similar to the process you went through when you applied for the mortgage to buy your home.

Here are the kinds of documents we need from you:

- two forms of identification
- verification that the property is your principal address

- signed application
- required legal documents
- property Insurance information
- statement(s) on any existing mortgage (if applicable)
- proof that your property taxes are up-to-date

Now that many of our clients are more technically savvy, we are doing more things electronically. For example, we accept digital document signatures. Generally, the entire process can take up to three to four weeks (although we have processed them more quickly if there is an urgent need), and a Mortgage Specialist is assigned to you to guide you every step of the way. After we approve the CHIP Reverse Mortgage and draw up the paperwork, we require you to seek independent legal advice, at your expense (this usually costs a few hundred dollars), to make sure that you have someone who is arms-length to advise you on whether the deal is right for you and to answer any final questions.

We have the independent legal counsel requirement in place so that the client feels very comfortable with their decision, and also to make sure that there is no undue influence from outside parties. For example, that the client is not being pressured to get a reverse mortgage by family members. Many people have a lawyer they trust already, and we also keep a list of independent lawyers in case new clients have no contacts themselves. A real estate lawyer or family lawyer is often a good choice. Chapter Six includes a Q&A with a lawyer who has advised on many reverse mortgages.

There is a closing fee charged by HomeEquity Bank. As of 2020 it is $1,795 for most clients (individual circumstances vary), which covers legal costs, administrative costs, discharging any prior mortgage and registration of the CHIP Reverse Mortgage. The closing fee is typically deducted from the proceeds of the reverse mortgage. Once the reverse mortgage is finalized, the funds are directly deposited into your account that week. Afterwards, we take the lead from clients in terms of follow-up. Our standard is to send an annual statement, but clients know they can call us any time.

Timely, courteous and personable service throughout. It was a pleasure conducting business with this agency.
- Gary

Rated on ★ Trustpilot

HomeEquity Bank

COSTS

It's important to know all the facts before getting into a reverse mortgage with HomeEquity Bank. Below, we will outline all the fees, interest rates and penalties you should be aware of. Your Mortgage Specialist will discuss them with you while going through the process, and they will also be explained during your independent legal advisor appointment before you sign the mortgage documents. Let's start with a breakdown of the fees we touched on above.

Fees

There are three types of fees you should expect when arranging for a reverse mortgage with HomeEquity Bank.

Appraisal fee – This fee is charged by a professional who will inspect and appraise your house and provide its estimated value. We use that value along with your age, location and type of property to determine how much money we can lend you. Appraisal fees vary based on where your property is located, but generally they run $300 to $600 per appraisal.

Mortgage fee – HomeEquity Bank will charge you a fee for arranging the CHIP Reverse Mortgage. Currently in 2020, the fee is $1,795 and it covers all our internal legal costs, title checks, title insurance and other miscellaneous costs. For the most part, our customers ask for the fee to be paid from the reverse mortgage. This fee is similar to a legal fee you would pay to the bank when arranging a conventional mortgage. Our other products may have different fees. Current fee information is always available on our website www.chip.ca.

Independent legal advisor (ILA) fee – This is a fee that you must pay to a third-party lawyer to get independent legal advice before you sign your mortgage papers with HomeEquity Bank. We have explained the reason for hiring the ILA—simply put, we want to make sure that our clients have an opportunity to speak with an independent party before making a financial decision in retirement. It provides peace of mind for us, for our clients and for their families. After all, a lot can change as people age, and some may not even remember some of the decisions and conversations from the past. ILA fees can range from $300 to $700 depending on how much your lawyer charges and if there is any other business you address while in the meeting.

Interest Rates

How are reverse mortgage rates calculated? As the leading provider of reverse mortgages in Canada, HomeEquity Bank works to ensure that the rates we offer our customers are competitive and fair. Many customers ask why the interest rates associated with a reverse mortgage are slightly higher than a conventional mortgage or line of credit. While there are many myths out there, the truth is there are a few important reasons why reverse mortgage interest rates may be higher.

Unlike a conventional mortgage and almost every other lending option, a reverse mortgage requires no regular principal or interest payments.

- With a conventional mortgage or line of credit, you are required to make monthly mortgage payments (and if you are unable to pay, you could go into default and risk losing your home).

- A reverse mortgage is a flexible financial solution. It will help you to have less cash outflow, and your monthly income will not be reduced by having to pay regular interest or principal payments. The amount you owe will only be due when you decide to move or sell.

- The reverse mortgage will also be "due" if the borrower

contravenes their mortgage terms or fails to meet their obligations under their reverse mortgage agreement.

With a reverse mortgage, you will never owe more than your home is worth. Think of it like built-in insurance for your retirement future.

- Due to our "No Negative Equity Guarantee," as long as the mortgage obligations are met, the amount you will have to repay on the due date will not exceed the fair market value of your home. HomeEquity Bank will assume the difference between the sale price and the loan amount.

- The guarantee excludes administrative expenses and interest that has accumulated after the due date.

The same funding sources that are available to banks for conventional mortgages are not available for reverse mortgages.

Certain programs administered by the federal government enable the banks to fund their conventional mortgage originations at a low cost. One of the key requirements for participation in such programs is that the mortgages must have periodic cash flows, which are collected with mortgage payments. Since reverse mortgages are designed so that borrowers do not have to make any payments for as long as the loan is outstanding, HomeEquity Bank cannot participate in such programs and, as a result, its funding costs are higher than the major Canadian banks.

Our rates may be slightly higher than that of a conventional mortgage, but the two products are very different and were each created to provide a different solution for Canadians. While a conventional mortgage is meant to help Canadians afford to buy a home, a reverse mortgage was primarily designed to help Canadians 55 and older access funds while retaining ownership and title of their house. It helps you get the cash you need to live a comfortable and secure retirement, without having to worry about regular mortgage payments.

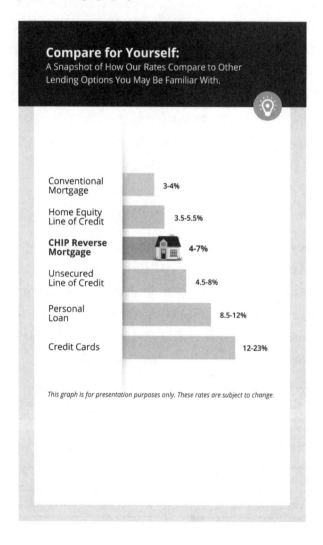

Compare for Yourself:
A Snapshot of How Our Rates Compare to Other Lending Options You May Be Familiar With.

Conventional Mortgage	3-4%
Home Equity Line of Credit	3.5-5.5%
CHIP Reverse Mortgage	4-7%
Unsecured Line of Credit	4.5-8%
Personal Loan	8.5-12%
Credit Cards	12-23%

This graph is for presentation purposes only. These rates are subject to change.

Types of Reverse Mortgage Interest Rates

CHIP Reverse Mortgage interest rates are available in two different formats: fixed term or variable term. Variable term rates are determined by the HomeEquity Bank prime rate, which tends to change when the Bank of Canada adjusts its benchmark rate. A variable rate may fluctuate up or down over the course of the term, which is why it is called "variable" and is not locked in for a particular term (unlike our fixed reset terms). A fixed-term rate, on the other hand, is set for a determined period, which is why it is called "fixed." The CHIP Reverse Mortgage fixed-term rates are available for a six-month, 1-year, 3-year or 5-year period. Clients typically prefer longer terms, such as the 5-year, but the choice is yours!

Pre-Payment Penalties

A reverse mortgage is typically a longer-term mortgage product, and most customers get the CHIP Reverse Mortgage to be able to stay in the home they love for as long as they can. If that sounds like you, and you are planning to stay in your home for five or more years, these penalties will not apply to you. That said, it's important to properly disclose them to all clients.

CHIP Reverse Mortgage Penalty Calculations	
Year 1	5%
Year 2	4%
Year 3	3%
Year 4 & Year 5	Three months' interest

There are pre-payment penalties on all types of mortgages, so if you have a conventional mortgage you are also subject to pre-payment penalties, and if you have a mortgage with non-bank lenders there may also be fees for paying back early. It's important to always ask questions and be educated.

In the event that our clients pass away and the property needs to be sold, we waive pre-payment penalties. In the event a client moves to a retirement home, we reduce pre-payment penalties by 50 percent. **We understand that life events can't be predicted, so it's important to us to offer some flexibility during difficult times.**

Our rates, fees and early repayment penalties are disclosed on our website. We see the CHIP Reverse Mortgage as a long-term product, for people who want to age in place and stay in the home they love. So, for many of our clients, early repayment is not something they are considering. Interest is charged until the loan is paid off, and the interest is added to the original loan amount, so that increases over time. If you move, you will have to pay back what's left on the loan.

WHAT PEOPLE BUY WITH A REVERSE MORTGAGE

When it comes to clients and their financial needs, there's a spectrum of reasons they want to borrow from us. Some need an extra reserve to help with living costs, such as property taxes or regular maintenance or even to pay an existing mortgage. They are looking for a plan that will help them keep money accessible so that those ongoing expenses don't add up. Others find themselves short of funds for a major expense, often an unexpected one like a leaky roof or a car that's broken down before its time. Sometimes they want to help their families with unexpected expenses.

Over the years, we have noticed that people use their money in six main ways:

1. **To take care of finances** – This could mean paying off a regular mortgage, credit cards, debts to family, etc.

2. **To pursue passions and interests** – Some clients start a new business, others want to travel.

3. **For gifting** – Financial gifts to adult children or grand-children can be very satisfying and can help them with everything from a down payment on a house to university tuition.

4. **For health expenses** – This is becoming more and more common, for small things like medication not covered by private plans to paying for in-home care.

5. **To do renovations** – There are two categories of renovations we see: lifestyle improvements and accessibility renovations.

6. **As an income supplement** – People take this option when they want to use their house as a pension plan, to draw a little bit of money every month to age in place and with dignity.

There are so many reasons for wanting a reverse mortgage, and you'll read about some of them in the client profiles in this book. The product is used for a variety of reasons. One client borrowed from us because her daughter hadn't saved enough money for her children's university tuition, and the grandmother didn't want to see her grandchildren graduate with student debt. Another client wanted money to help her daughter through a messy divorce. Another wanted the cash to be able to take advantage of an investment opportunity. Some have a dream that they want to bring to reality, such as a kitchen renovation or a bucket-list trip (or several) that they're dreaming of taking. One of our clients took a trip of a lifetime to Spain, at 86 years old! He was delighted to be able to make this lifelong travel dream come true. Another wanted to meet her grandchildren who live across the country. Some clients are just tired of feeling so pinched that they can't go out once a week for wings or have a "date night" with their spouse once a month.

While our clients all have the excellent investment of their homes in common, some also feel really stuck due to unfortunate circumstances. One client said that she'd only bought food from the dollar store for several months because she couldn't afford anything more expensive. We have helped a number of clients to pay for their dental work and to get hearing aids. Some clients have had gambling debts to pay off. These clients have often turned to more expensive loans with high interest rates, like second mortgages, unsecured loans, private loans or even credit cards with interest rates as high as 19 or 23 percent and hefty fees. For them, we offer a pathway through the debt that turns the benefits of their biggest asset into a way out of that stress and anxiety.

And while the examples we just gave you cover a wide range of product uses, the one that continues to be the most common is number one on our list: taking care of personal finances and paying off other debt. Many people are surprised to learn that almost 15 percent of Canadians who are 65 or older are carrying conventional mortgages in retirement at an average mortgage size of $110,000. It can be especially surprising in cases where they purchased their homes in the mid-1960s for $20,000 to $50,000. How can this be? Our clients tell us that life got in the way: things like unexpected expenses, job losses, children (they can be expensive), poor investment choices, no savings and sometimes health problems at a later age. Some feel shame that they are not in a better financial situation. Many hide it from their families, including their children.

If you have a $110,000 conventional mortgage on your property, your monthly mortgage payments (at a 2 percent interest rate) are approximately $450 per month. Such low payments may seem attractive to someone younger with great employment income, but to an older person on a fixed income, it can be financially devastating. Recently, we arranged a CHIP Max mortgage for a couple in their seventies with a $718,000 conventional mortgage on their property (under a 25-year amortization), where their monthly mortgage payments were over $3,000—and they live on a fixed income. Fortunately, their Toronto house is worth more than $1.5 million, and so the CHIP Reverse Mortgage was the right option. Here's a direct quote from their email to us: "I'm going to have an emotional breakdown . . . Please, I beg, help me out."

While reverse mortgages may not be for everyone, we at HomeEquity Bank believe they provide a great option for some. Why? Because it's needed. Government pensions are not enough to sustain us through retirement, many people have insufficient savings and most of us don't have the luxury of company pension plans. Owning our house provides an opportunity to use the equity as part of a comprehensive financial retirement plan.

HOME APPRECIATION STORIES

Another concern we hear quite often about reverse mortgages is that you will not have any money left in your home after you've paid your loan. People worry that, since the interest rate is slightly higher, it will eat up all the equity and there will be nothing left over for them later in life. Worse yet, they worry that there will be no inheritance. This is a myth.

There are two approaches when it comes to explaining home appreciation scenarios: one is to do it with numbers, and the other way is to explain through storytelling. Our preference is to start by telling you two stories from our top Mortgage Specialists, who convey them directly to the hundreds of clients they work with every year. We will illustrate these stories with graphs.

Home Appreciation Story 1

Imagine you own a house worth $600,000 and you decide to take out a CHIP Reverse Mortgage. You get a $100,000 initial advance at a 5-year mortgage term rate of 4.59 percent.

- At the end of the year, the interest that has accumulated is $4,590. You have the option of paying that interest off or, what most people do, to defer paying it until the house is sold.

- At the end of the same year, your friendly neighbourhood realtor stops by and tells you that your property has increased in value by 3 percent in the past 12 months.

- That percentage can vary, but believe me, in Canada 3 percent is conservative: the Canadian Real Estate Association numbers show a higher 5 percent annual appreciation over a 15-year period. Of course, there are periods of time when it's closer to 0 percent, just as there are times when it's closer to 10 percent. So, to be conservative, let's use 3 percent. This means that at the end of the first year, your house is worth $618,000.

Simple math will show you that you are actually ahead: You gained $18,000 in house value and your interest cost is only $4,590, for a net of $13,420. If you repeat the scenario for 10 years, you will end up with a house worth over $800,000, an original CHIP Reverse Mortgage balance of $100,000 and $62,000 in interest, leaving you with whopping $643,000 in home equity! Remember, all this time you are living in the home you love, and the value continues to increase.

Steven, here is a summary of what your reverse mortgage and home equity could look like over time.

	Today	In 10 Years
Home Value	$600,000	$806,350
Reverse Mortgage	$100,000	$100,000
Interest	$0	$62,507
Remaining Home Equity	$500,000	$643,843

After **10 Years** you could have **$643,843** remaining in home equity.

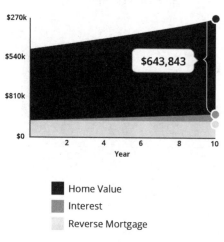

HomeEquity Bank reverse mortgage evaluation for Story 1

Yvonne, here is a summary of what your reverse mortgage and home equity could look like over time.

	Today	In 20 Years
Home Value	$350,000	$1,631,335
Reverse Mortgage	$75,000	$75,000
Interest	$0	$132,959
Remaining Home Equity	$275,000	$1,423,376

After **20 Years** you could have **$1,423,376** remaining in home equity.

HomeEquity Bank reverse mortgage evaluation for Story 2

Home Appreciation Story 2

The first "story" was more of a scenario, but now we're going to tell you an actual story, and it doesn't have a happy ending. Let's go back to the year 2000 and look at a couple, both in their sixties, living in Mississauga, Ontario. Both have health problems, and their future is looking bleak. It's hard for them to look after the house, their finances are overwhelming, and their four adult children are busy raising their young families. The couple decides to sell the house, get all the equity out, pay off all their debts and rent a modest apartment. The house is sold for $350,000, and when their $75,000 in debts and fees are paid, they are left with approximately $275,000. They are thinking that in their poor health they will have 10 years to live off the $275,000 and some pension income, paying $1,250 per month for rent.

Fast-forward to 2020, they are both alive, albeit frailer than ever. Their rent is now $2,500 per month and the money from the house sale is long gone. Their four adult children are now splitting their parents' living costs four ways, paying rent at $625 per month each. A new toaster is split four ways, the cost of a wheelchair is split four ways, weekly groceries are split four ways—you get the picture. The four adult children are working to support their parents, themselves and their families.

The worst part, the part that truly underlines the sad ending, is that the house in Mississauga that they sold for $350,000 back in 2000 sold last year for $1.5 million. Imagine how different their life would be if they stayed put. They would be comfortable; they could have got more money over time as the value of the property kept increasing *and* there would have been inheritance. It's a true story.

In the attached graphic that summarizes Story 2, we include most of the facts of this story so you can see it visually: the $350,000 initial value of the house, the $75,000 financial need, an appreciation at 8 percent (sounds like they bought the right house) and a 20-year time horizon. You may find it hard to believe, but if they had taken out a CHIP Reverse Mortgage back in 2000, the interest accumulated and compounded over time would add up to approximately $132,000 and the home equity would have continued to grow. There would be $1.4 million for the four adult children as an inheritance.

We hope this section provided a powerful confirmation that there will still be good value in your home when you choose a reverse mortgage. You may also see why we love numbers so much! They really cut through some of the misconceptions and allow you to focus on your own situation.

Because we all can see the reality of how the housing market has grown over the past decades. The increase in house prices across Canada, and especially in major urban centres, means housing continues to be a smart, amazing investment. Even in the midst of the pandemic, the Canadian Real Estate Association noted in September 2020 that the average price of a Canadian resale home was $604,000, up 17.5 percent from the average price a year earlier. Many Canadians already think of their home as a key part of their retirement strategy, an investment that will augment any pension they may receive.

In our changing economy, HomeEquity Bank has seen even more uptake of the CHIP Reverse Mortgage product in recent years. HomeEquity Bank originated $833 million in new reverse mortgages in 2020, marking a record year for the company and demonstrating that more Canadians are seeing the value in this product. With the massive changes in the economy since 2008 and again in 2020, retirees might have less money than they expected when originally planning their retirement. It's not as if you can liquidate a bedroom or a bathroom or, say, sell off just a part of your home. But the reverse mortgage allows you to do that, in a way, to get this value from something that you already own.

COMMON MYTHS AND MISCONCEPTIONS

While reverse mortgages have been offered in Canada for over 30 years, there are still some myths, misconceptions and mistruths related to the product. It's hard to guess where they started and how they persist. There were some issues with reverse mortgages (called Home Equity Conversion Mortgages or HECMs) in the United States, and since stories always spill over the border, people might think Canada is the same. But even in the United States the situation has improved, and yet people still have concerns that are just based on bad information, or "fake news" as we call it today.

While it's hard to address the United States specifically, it is important to remember that in Canada, HomeEquity Bank is federally regulated and therefore subject to regulatory oversight.

We are frequently reviewed, and our practices and products are regularly audited. In Canada, the banking industry is closely regulated compared with other countries, and this oversight spells greater protection for Canadians.

Because knowledge is power, we'd like to tackle some of the biggest myths about our reverse mortgages. And we'll also ask for your help: if you hear some of these myths coming from the mouths of other people (the worst is when we hear them from people who could really benefit from considering the reverse mortgage), please speak up and correct their misinformation. It's really harming older Canadians who need the correct facts to make an informed decision.

Okay, let's get on with busting those myths. Why not start with a quiz? We invite you to test your knowledge to see how well you understand the product. Ready? Grab a pen or pencil and circle your responses below. Let's go:

REVERSE MORTGAGE QUIZ

1. Canadians must be at least 55 years of age and be homeowner(s) in order to enter into a reverse mortgage. **True/False**

2. With a reverse mortgage, the homeowner is not required to repay the loan until he/she stops using the home as their principal residence. **True/False**

3. You cannot enter into a reverse mortgage unless your

home is completely mortgage free. **True/False**

4. One downside of a reverse mortgage is that if the home is worth less than the amount owed to the lender, then the homeowner, estate or heirs need to pay off the additional debt. **True/False**

5. The only available type of payment from a reverse mortgage is a single lump-sum distribution. **True/False**

6. With a reverse mortgage, you can borrow up to 55 percent of the value of your home, and that percentage depends on the age of the borrower(s), the location and value of the home, and the type of property. **True/False**

7. A reverse mortgage differs from a traditional mortgage in that the homeowner is not responsible for any property taxes or insurance payments. **True/False**

8. Once your reverse mortgage loan is approved, you can remain in the home, but the lender becomes the owner of your home. **True/False**

9. The use of reverse mortgage funds is restricted to health expenditures, long-term care costs and tax payments. **True/False**

10. With a reverse mortgage, government benefits such as Old Age Security (OAS), Canada Pension Plan (CPP) or the Guaranteed Income Supplement (GIS) may be affected. **True/False**

Myths Debunked

How did you do on the quiz? For your convenience, we're including the answers right here, along with some corrections.

REVERSE MORTGAGE QUIZ ANSWERS

1. Canadians must be at least 55 years of age and be homeowner(s) in order to enter into a reverse mortgage. <u>TRUE</u>/False

    The reality? Yes, these are the requirements. (Don't forget that all people who live in the home must be 55 or older to qualify for the CHIP Reverse Mortgage).

2. With a reverse mortgage, the homeowner is not required to repay the loan until he/she stops using the home as the principal residence. <u>TRUE</u>/False

    The reality? You are not required to pay a cent until the home is sold, as long as you abide by the terms of your agreement.

3. You cannot enter into a reverse mortgage unless your home is completely mortgage free. True/<u>FALSE</u>

    The reality? You must consolidate existing mortgages using the reverse mortgage.

4. One downside of a reverse mortgage is that if the home is worth less than the amount owed to the lender, then the homeowner, estate or heirs need to pay off the additional

debt. True/**FALSE**

The reality? HomeEquity Bank's conservative lending approach means that 99 percent of our clients have equity remaining in their home after it's sold.

5.   The only available type of payment from a reverse mortgage is a single lump-sum distribution. True/**FALSE**

The reality? Many clients take their reverse mortgage out in partial advances or use our Income Advantage product for regular cash flow.

6.   With a reverse mortgage, you can borrow up to 55 percent of the value of your home, and that percentage depends on the age of the borrower(s), the location and value of the home, and the type of property. **TRUE**/False

The reality? Yes, these are the factors. To find out what you qualify for, contact one of our Mortgage Specialists to discuss your specific situation.

7.   A reverse mortgage differs from a traditional mortgage in that the homeowner is not responsible for any property taxes or insurance payments. True/**FALSE**

The reality? A condition of your reverse mortgage is that you keep up your tax payments, insurance and property upkeep.

8.   Once your reverse mortgage loan is approved, you can remain in the home, but the lender becomes the owner of your home. True/**FALSE**

The reality? Your name always remains on the title of your home.

9. The use of reverse mortgage funds is restricted to health expenditures, long-term care costs and tax payments. True/**FALSE**

   The reality? You can use the reverse mortgage to cover any costs you wish. Many clients also use the money for home renovations, travel, gifts to their family and more!

10. With a reverse mortgage, government benefits such as Old Age Security (OAS), Canada Pension Plan (CPP) or the Guaranteed Income Supplement (GIS) may be affected. True/**FALSE**

    The reality? The reverse mortgage does not affect these government benefits.

" Since I completed my transaction, my life has changed for the better in every way, even my health, but most of all my feeling of security. For that I am most grateful. "

- J. Sanlon

Rated on ★ Trustpilot   HomeEquity Bank ☰

REVERSE MORTGAGE SCENARIOS ACROSS THE COUNTRY

How Much Cash Can You Access?

You might be a person who wants to see the numbers, and who can blame you? So, we ran a few scenarios for you, to show you how much money you can qualify for (that's another of our top questions) when you take out a reverse mortgage at various ages.

Toronto, ON: $800,000 detached home (the average Toronto price at the end of 2019 was $819, 319)

Age	Male	Female	Same-age couple
55	$204,000–$261,000	$230,000–$286,000	$184,000–240,000
65	$275,000–$335,000	$282,000–$338,000	$232,000–$289,000
75	$378,000–$400,000	$348,000–$400,000	$334,000–$387,000
85+	$400,000–$440,000	$400,000–$440,000	$400,000–$440,000

Dartmouth, NS: $350,000 detached home

Age	Male	Female	Same-age couple
55	$92,000–$109,000	$103,000–$118,000	$83,000–$94,000
65	$125,000–$143,000	$126,000–$136,000	$104,000–$125,000
75	$169,000–$193,000	$156,000–$189,000	$149,000–$185,000
85+	$193,000	$193,000	$193,000

Calgary, AB: $450,000 semi-detached home

Age	Male	Female	Same-age couple
55	$112,000–$142,000	$125,000–$156,000	$101,000–$131,000
65	$152,000–$182,000	$153,000–$183,000	$126,000–$157,000
75	$205,000–$232,000	$189,000–$217,000	$181,000–$210,000
85+	$234,000	$234,000	$234,000

Vancouver, BC: $600,000 condo

Age	Male	Female	Same-age couple
55	$141,000–$179,000	$158,000–$197,000	$127,000–$165,000
65	$192,000–$230,000	$194,000–$232,000	$160,000–$198,000
75	$259,000–$293,000	$239,000–$275,000	$229,000–$265,000
85+	$297,000	$297,000	$297,000

OTHER HOMEEQUITY BANK PRODUCTS

While the CHIP Reverse Mortgage is HomeEquity Bank's flagship product, we have developed a few others that help to meet more specific needs, from the need for regular cash flow to the need for greater borrowing. Here are your other options:

Income Advantage

Our Income Advantage product is ideal for those looking to supplement their monthly income and to cover expenses. You can start by taking out a small lump sum (the minimum initial advance is $20,000), plus you can receive more money in monthly or quarterly deposits. Funds are disbursed starting at $1,000 monthly or $3,000 quarterly and can be increased to meet your needs. Or you can skip taking out a lump sum and just sign up for monthly deposits that best suit your needs. With Income Advantage, your house becomes your pension plan. This product involves the same application process and assessment as the CHIP Reverse Mortgage, requires no monthly payment and is still a loan secured against the value in your home. The only difference is the distribution—this product provides regular cash flow to boost your day-to-day lifestyle.

CHIP Max

Our CHIP Max product provides borrowers with a loan amount up to 30 percent higher than the original CHIP Reverse Mortgage. The loan is still secured against the value of your home, requires no monthly payment and involves the same application process as the CHIP Reverse Mortgage. This product is only available in urban centres in Alberta, British Columbia, Ontario and Quebec.

CHIP Open

The CHIP Open is a newer product designed for those who want more flexibility to repay their mortgage sooner. We developed it based on customer feedback, and it is well-timed for the uncertainties of a pandemic or other crises. CHIP Open provides you with an option to pay back your CHIP Open faster than our flagship product, with no pre-payment penalties. For that reason, the interest rate is higher for CHIP Open than it is for a CHIP Reverse Mortgage, but clients have told us that they want and value flexibility. While we started working on the product before the pandemic hit, the timing couldn't have been more perfect: people want and need to have options. We have seen a very positive response to this new product.

CHIPReverseMortgage™

PURPOSE

Our most popular product type, the **CHIP Reverse Mortgage** is ideal for homeowners 55+ who are looking for a **one-time lump sum**

BEST USED FOR

 Paying off stressful debt

 Renovations which could increase your home's value

 A large expense (health, car or helping family)

ELIGIBILITY

 Canadian Homeowners

 Borrower(s) must be 55+

 The home must be your primary residence

Which program is right for you? Let's compare your options.

PURPOSE

Designed for homeowners aged 55-75, **CHIP MAX** can provide clients in select locations a **loan amount up to 30% more** than that of a CHIP Reverse Mortgage

BEST USED FOR

 Avoiding high-interest loans or an additional mortgage

 Boosting your income

 Loan consolidation

ELIGIBILITY

 Canadian Homeowners

 Borrower(s) must be 55+

 The home must be your primary residence

Which program is right for you? Let's compare your options.

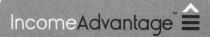

PURPOSE

Created for homeowners looking to supplement their retirement income, **Income Advantage provides monthly advances** in addition to a one-time lump sum

BEST USED FOR

(+) Boosting your day-to-day lifestyle

Increasing monthly cashflow

Protecting your investments

ELIGIBILITY

Canadian Homeowners

(55+) Borrower(s) must be 55+

The home must be your primary residence

Which program is right for you? Let's compare your options.

CHIP Open™

PURPOSE

Made for homeowners searching for a **short-term financial solution**, who are willing to pay a higher interest rate and closing fee in lieu of any prepayment penalties

BEST USED FOR

 Bridge financing or as a short-term cashflow solution

 Avoiding high prepayment penalties

 Flexibility to convert to longer-term solution

ELIGIBILITY

 Canadian Homeowners

 Borrower(s) must be 55+

 The home must be your primary residence

Which program is right for you? Let's compare your options.

DECIDE FOR YOURSELF: PROS AND CONS OF THE CHIP REVERSE MORTGAGE

There are several factors to consider before deciding to proceed with a reverse mortgage. As with any big decision, it's helpful to speak to family and friends and ensure that you fully understand the pros and cons of the reverse mortgage in Canada. Here are some of those pros and cons as we see them:

Pros:

- You receive the reverse mortgage funds as tax-free cash, and you can spend the money any way you like!

- You stay in the home you love and maintain ownership and control of your home. All you have to do is maintain your property and pay your property taxes and homeowner's insurance.

- There are no monthly mortgage payments required until you decide to move or sell your home.

- The CHIP Reverse Mortgage is a non-recourse loan, which means that at the time of repayment, you (or your estate) will never owe more than the fair market value of your home—as long as you have maintained your property taxes and insurance.

- You can choose how to receive the funds from the CHIP Reverse Mortgage. You can receive it all at once in a lump sum or in scheduled advances over time—it's up to you!

Cons:

- Because there are no monthly mortgage payments required, interest rates for the CHIP Reverse Mortgage tend to be higher than that of a traditional mortgage option.

- The balance of the loan increases over time, as does the interest on the loan.

We promised at the beginning of this chapter that it would provide more detail than you may ever have read in one place about the CHIP Reverse Mortgage, and hopefully you have a good understanding now. However, if you ever have questions about reverse mortgages, please don't hesitate to visit our website at www.chip.ca, call our contact centre at 1-833-357-2447 or speak to your banker, mortgage broker or financial advisor. We really think that discussing the specifics of your situation can help you evaluate even more clearly whether the product is right to you and your retirement planning. So, what are you waiting for? Give us a call!

EXPERT SPOTLIGHT: DR. THOMAS DAVIDOFF, UNIVERSITY OF BRITISH COLUMBIA

"It depends on the person, but [the reverse mortgage] is a pretty amazing product. You're allowing yourself flexibility and insuring against longevity—because if you happen to live a long time, you're likely to have made more money on this than you're ever going to pay back. And if your home value plummets, you've made money on it. So, you're getting insurance against a lot of important things. And you have this giant illiquid source of wealth. I mean, you have all these cash-poor, house-rich people in Canada, in retirement. It's a great way to pay your bills, in principle, and an absolutely fantastic product. It would be great if it could be expanded. With low interest rates, the ratio of housing equity to lifetime wealth is going to just get larger."

Dr. Thomas Davidoff is Director of the UBC Centre for Urban Economics and Real Estate and an associate professor of Strategy and Business Economics at the University of British Columbia's Sauder School of Business. Dr. Davidoff's areas of expertise include housing, aging, insurance and mortgages. He has written several articles on the topic of reverse mortgages.

EXPERT SPOTLIGHT: DUSTAN WOODHOUSE

Dustan Woodhouse is president of Mortgage Architects (www.mortgagearchitects.ca), a national mortgage brokerage. He is also author of several successful books on topics related to mortgages.

What do you think of the reverse mortgage product?

Of the 1,695 mortgages I've arranged, only one was a reverse mortgage. It's the most misunderstood product in Canada, an absolute nightmare to try and explain it. Kids think they're stealing the parents' inheritance, and clients think they're going to lose the equity in their home. After the one, I've pointed clients in the direction of HomeEquity Bank.

This product is for everybody, accessible to everybody. Anyone and everyone who has equity in a home stands to benefit from this. And the Income Advantage product? That's a no-brainer. Think about people in Vancouver or Toronto who are retired. Did you know that over 50 percent of homes in BC are clear title? Fifty percent of homes in the entire province have no mortgage whatsoever.

Perception-wise, everybody always thinks that in Vancouver, everybody's mortgaged up to the gills. Not the case. I mean, property values are high, but lots and lots of people bought-in five years ago, 10 years ago, 20, 25 years ago. So, the majority have significant equity in their homes.

How do you think people should use the product?

So, you look at the average home price being over a million dollars, and you drop two thousand bucks a month out of that—you'd have to live forever to really catch up to the equity limit. And an extra two thousand bucks a month is a game changer for an awful lot of people. Even $500 a month or $1,000 a month, just that little top up.

My own folks are in their mid-seventies. And they make comments like, "We can't really afford a new car. We can't afford a cruise," or whatever. And I'm like, "You're in a $1.3 million house. Draw out one thousand bucks a month and go on a cruise every quarter! Draw out one thousand bucks a month and drive a brand-new BMW." It's like, you're not going to actually impact your situation. The women in my family live to be a hundred. So, okay, Mom, you got 25 more years to go? One thousand bucks a month out of your home that's worth $1.3 million? Which, 25 years from now, will be worth $2.5 million?

Why do you think the reverse mortgage product is not better recognized?

I think that the overwhelming challenge is this—and I see it in all generations—we've been raised with this mentality that all debt is bad debt. And the number-one goal in life is to pay off your house and never, ever, ever borrow against your home. Because if you can't make the payments, you'll lose your home. That mentality is exceedingly damaging to a lot of people. I mean, it's why you have, you know, people living in their homes eating cat food, struggling.

There's a totally inaccurate stigma attached to the product. And so, it's not being advised as much as it should be advised. Because it's an uphill battle to advise on it. So, a lot of mortgage brokers, a lot of professionals in the banking industry, shy away from promoting this product.

Do you think the perception has changed at all over the years?

I think the understanding of this product has shifted perhaps 1 percent over the years. The pace has been glacial. I looked at the numbers, and holistically it should have vastly higher numbers. Because there's no question that there are seniors living on ridiculously tight budgets. And in homes that are worth hundreds of thousands, or in some cases, millions of dollars, with just no clue that they could even access that $1,000 or $2,000 a month, and it would totally change things.

The one client I had that I arranged the reverse mortgage for, I think about all the time. They took up to $4,000 a month, and that allowed them to pay for a full-time, live-in caretaker. And they stayed in their home probably eight years longer than they would have otherwise. I recommend the reverse mortgage to everybody. I talk about it all the time, but I talk about it in the context of "too bad more people aren't using this."

CHAPTER THREE

PORTRAIT OF THE NEW RETIREE

While I had never really focused my career on any particular demographic, let alone the 55-plus group, when I arrived at HomeEquity Bank to take up my first role as Senior Vice President of Marketing and Sales, I instantly realized that this age group deserved more attention. To begin with, it's a demographic that makes up a huge number of people in Canada! According to Statistics Canada, by July 2020, over 6.8 million adults in Canada were over the age of 65. By 2021, one in five people will be 65 or older, and one in three will be over the age of 55. More thoughtfully, is there a better group to champion than the men and women who blazed the trails that have allowed us to live the life we are enjoying now? I realized that working for them would serve as a deeper mission for my own career and for who I am as a person.

The inspiration I draw both from the people I work with and the people we serve was refreshed once again when the COVID-19 pandemic hit Canada. The first thought on everyone's mind at HomeEquity Bank was to wonder how our customers were doing. After all, the average age of our customers is 72, so some of them are in age groups that the medical community reported to be more vulnerable to the virus. But how to check in on them? Well, how were we keeping in touch with our own family and friends? By giving them a friendly call. So, that's what we decided to do with our customers. We divided up the client contact list and called it Operation Warm Hug.

Our chats were a big success. Many clients told us our call was both a surprise and a gesture they really appreciated. We were glad to hear they were okay and doing what we were doing: things like reading, preparing to start their spring planting in the garden and catching up on some home organization projects. Many of our staff were touched that our customers asked us how we were doing, too. It's the kind of connection that happens a lot around here.

As the economy grew increasingly unstable during the pandemic, many new clients also reached out to us. They began to see potential financial challenges in their future, but they knew that their investment in their homes remained solid. Like many of us, having to shelter in place made them feel grateful that they are fortunate to have good homes as a base to do just that. However shocking and disruptive the pandemic may have been when it hit, it reminded us that our homes are our sanctuaries.

CONNECTING WITH CLIENTS

A recurring topic of conversation in our Operation Warm Hug calls was the connection that our clients have to their homes. Like most of us in the spring of 2020, these folks were locked down and making the best of it. We also discussed the worrisome news about the spread of the virus within the country's long-term care homes. As it turned out, studies by the Canadian Institute for Health Information released in May 2020 showed that long-term care residents made up 81 percent of all reported COVID-19 deaths in the country compared to an average of 42 percent in the other OECD countries studied. The other countries ranged from less than 10 percent in Slovenia and Hungary to 66 percent in Spain.

Happy HomeEquity Bank client David Holmes.

Thankfully, our customers had already decided years ago that they valued the security and familiarity of the homes where they'd spent so many years. That's part of the reason they became customers, to keep their homes. As we all waited out the pandemic in our homes in those early days, our clients felt that security even more. It reaffirmed their decision to "age in place," even though they also expressed their support for future reforms to the long-term care system.

When people ask us about our average customer, we respond that they are, by requirement, 55-plus homeowners, but after that they are remarkably diverse. They live in the city and the country, and they have homes ranging from a semi-detached in Toronto to a townhouse in Calgary. Some love to travel, and others love nothing more than staying home to work on their back garden. Some are single, some are couples, some have big families and others have no kids. They all have many different financial situations. Some come to us to liquidate cash from a multimillion-dollar house, and others are looking for solutions to debt problems.

So, when we look to paint a portrait of the new retiree, we're well aware that the demographic does not have a single face. That said, as a cohort they do share some new realities of aging. But when we think of the people we've spoken to over the years, they seem more active, more technologically savvy and more community engaged than the stereotype of the older adult that's become all too common. These are not people ready to sit back and watch the world from their front porch. They're volunteering, some are still in the workforce and they're socially active.

CLIENT SPOTLIGHT: SUSAN STEWART

We've sprinkled a handful of Q&As with inspirational clients through-out the book to provide a sampling of the real voices behind people who have chosen the reverse mortgage.

What was your route to the reverse mortgage?

I've just turned 70, but can I say I'm a pretty young 70? I've got all my capabilities and I'm active. But costs are going up, and I don't want to move from my condo. I live in Coquitlam, which is part of the lower Vancouver mainland. And I'd have to move farther out. I don't want to move because I have better access to my children and grandchildren where I am now. But I was feeling quite strained with keeping up with everything. I want to be able to give my grandchildren some little treats, a little bit of money here and there.

I'm in the Lower Mainland, so property value doesn't go down. It's a good investment, any kind of property. I think by the time I'll be done with this place, I will have tripled my money. I'm on my own, which I really like—I don't want to be with a partner. But I do not want to have to worry about money, as far as treating the grandkids or buying the better piece of meat or being able to go out for coffee with the girls.

I do a lot of volunteer work, and that costs because you get together with your girlfriends, too. It's such a worthy cause. We help young women or old women, part of the Optimists. I like to be a member, and that costs a little bit.

I've tightened my belt. I had a little cash part-time job where I looked after a friend's children about three days a week. Since the pandemic hit, I don't have that cash anymore, that little bit of spending money. I wanted to take my anxiety away, so that I could still stay in my condo, I could still stay independent. I live very modestly, but it's just the cost of everything is so incredibly high.

How are you using your reverse mortgage money?

I'm still able to treat my grandchildren. And when I say treat, it's nothing big. This year, two of them graduated. They go to the States for their education because they have scholarships in lacrosse. And I also wanted to take a trip, not a cruise or anything like that, but a driving trip. I don't want to have to worry about if I have enough money to do that. So, taking out a CHIP Reverse Mortgage has just relieved my stress. It makes for healthier living for me. I had developed high blood pressure; I was so stressed.

I want to go back to the Northwest Territories because I lived there for several years. And it's a beautiful drive in summer, because the sun doesn't set. I'll just see my old girlfriends and have a wonderful visit. I happen to love driving. So, I want to do this while I'm healthy. And another trip I would like to take is to see the east coast of the United States with a friend, either a bus tour or maybe we will fly somewhere and then rent a car. We can share the costs.

What was your experience with HomeEquity Bank?

I went to see my person at the Toronto Dominion Bank, and I was trying to work out how I could lower my mortgage rate. Just trying to figure out a way of being able to have a few hundred more dollars a month, maybe $400 or so, just so I can pay the bills. Right now, the insurance bill is coming up. Insurance is crazy out here in BC. I get the top rate of 40 percent off, and I'm still paying $1,700 dollars for car insurance. That's a killer. And then, of course, along with it, there's health insurance and everything. Everything is so high out here. The people I dealt with at HomeEquity Bank were wonderful. My rep came in from Langley to my bank. She said, "Here's my card. Call me anytime." It was a very positive, great experience. Great people.

What has it meant to you to get a CHIP Reverse Mortgage?

I've had my reverse mortgage almost a year and I've been in my condo coming up on 12 years. It's just taken huge pressure off. We have been fortunate—my daughters have been able to manage and have never come to me for any large amount of money or anything like that—but this is a way of knowing that I can still be a good parent if something happened. A HomeEquity Bank reverse mortgage has given me peace of mind and freedom. And contentment. I look out and think, this is nice. I don't have to move from here.

Can you describe your family support?

I live about eight minutes from my daughter. I go up the hill to see her. She gets a lot of snow, but I'm down in the valley, so snow is not an issue. My daughters are now Lower Mainland girls. One is 47 and the other one is 50. They're very well-established here. One works in real estate and the other has a business with her husband.

I have four grandchildren. The oldest is 22 and the youngest is 14. And I love being able to give them memories, help them out a little bit here and there. And they know they can come to me and say, "Hey, Grams—what do you think of this idea?" I hate saying, "No, I can't afford it." But it's all within reason. It's amazing, that extra hundred dollars here and there, what it helps them with. I also have a cat. I'm a cat person. And he has some special food because he had crystals in his urine. He's healthy, but you know, if anything ever happens, it's an easy $400 to $700 bill from the vet.

Can you describe your condo?

I'm on the fourth floor and I overlook the mountains. I can people-watch. Since I moved in, there are 11 new high-rises that I can see from my sundeck, from my home. We're like this little jewel in the middle of these high-rises. I come out here at night and I look at all the lights. I get up early in the morning sometimes and watch the sun come up, watch the city wake up. I have a very large sundeck that wraps around my den and my great room. The deck winds all the way around three sliding glass doors and opens into my bedroom. I have probably one of the nicer decks in all of Coquitlam. I've got my rhubarb plants out here. I can sit out. I can see my neighbours walking with their pets, and we all wave to each other. It's really wonderful and it's very safe.

What's your neighbourhood like?

I live in a beautiful city—Coquitlam. The weather is nice. I'm within walking distance to anything you'd want. A big mall, grocery stores, and now they've built all these large high-rises around, but the lower level is all little stores. There's dentists and hairdressers and green-grocers and restaurants. We have an open area in the shape of a horseshoe, and you can go and sit down there in the sun.

There's a seniors' centre a block from me, and city hall is across the street. In the winter, they've got all their lights on and it's very beautiful. I've got something called LaFarge Lake, a man-made little lake. Everybody goes for a walk around it, and in the winter there's this huge Christmas display. If I want yoga, it's right here, and there's an aquarium centre that I like. And a spa with a hot tub, sauna, swimming, a wave pool. My church is eight minutes away. I don't really need to drive anywhere to get anything.

It's a really a very beautiful place to live. I'm glad I'm not down some street where nothing's happening. If I want to go for a little drive, you can drive down the valley to where they grow the corn and there there's all sorts of great places to buy food. I like where I live. I don't want to move. And the CHIP Reverse Mortgage has given me the opportunity to stay where I want to be. I feel I'm going to live here forever.

BRING ON THE BOOMERS

Today, many of our customers are of the generation known as the baby boomers. These boomers are the generation of people born after World War II, officially between 1946 and 1965. Of the over 6.8 million seniors in Canada, more than one in two were born in the boomer era. In the shadow of World War II, the baby boomer generation was born to parents who were marrying at a greater rate and a younger age (in their early twenties) and starting to have more children. The annual birth rate in Canada rose from 253,000 in 1940 to as high as 470,000 in 1960. Over 25 years, there were 1.5 million more births than usual—an increase of more than 18 percent for a total of around 8.6 million boomers.

It was an era of economic prosperity, progress and change. Suburbs expanded to meet the increased needs for affordable housing. The automobile saw mass-market adoption. Television was widely introduced into homes, changing family leisure time and increasing exposure to popular culture. Popular shows included *Howdy Doody, The Mickey Mouse Club, I Love Lucy, Bonanza, The Andy Griffith Show, The Ed Sullivan Show* and *Gilligan's Island*. Shows like *Leave It to Beaver* portrayed an idealized nuclear family, which influenced social norms about family life, with the male breadwinner as a common boomer model and a prevailing norm that mothers would engage in unpaid roles of homemaking and child raising.

By 1965, factors like the birth control pill, women entering the workforce in greater numbers and other changing realities, including the political upheaval of the decade, ended the baby boom. Boomers became teenagers between the 1960s and 1980s and grew up during a time of dramatic social change, including the Vietnam War, the counterculture of the 1960s, the Civil Rights movement and the Apollo 11 moon landing. In Canada, moments like the Centennial celebrations of 1967 ushered in new optimism for the country, while incidents like the October Crisis in Quebec, which led to the invocation of the War Measures Act in the 1970s, unsettled the nation's sense of security.

CLIENT SPOTLIGHT: JOHN AGIUS

We've sprinkled a handful of Q&As with inspirational clients throughout the book to provide a sampling of the real voices behind people who have chosen the reverse mortgage.

When did you decide to apply for a reverse mortgage?

Back in 2012, my parents were not well and in long-term care, and we needed some kind of loan to keep things in order as well as pay bills, now with long-term care. My former business partner had absconded with millions of dollars and had put me into

HomeEquity Bank client and musical talent John Agius.

bankruptcy a few years prior to 2012, so I had gone from triple-A to a delinquent credit rating overnight because of this criminal partner.

Where is your home and what do you like about it?

We are right in downtown Toronto, near Queen and Bathurst, in an old Victorian row house. The house is fairly long and somewhat narrow, like 16 feet wide. It is the centre home of three homes that were built together. It was built in 1912. I've converted the living room into my music studio. There are a lot of memories all over the place, in the dining room or in the basement or upstairs. It's a three-bedroom home.

When we first moved in there, I was eight years old. I moved away when I turned 20, then I came back when my parents got older. I'm 63 now. So, there's a ton of memories there. What can I tell you? Everybody wants to live on cool Queen West. It serves as my little bastion of a castle when I get home. I mean, it's a nightmare driving through downtown. But once I get home, I am home, and it's a very good home.

Outside of paying bills, what else have you done with the money?

We've done some minor renovations, navigated some other repairs. It's been helpful in that sense, that I can ask for a subsequent loan if I need one. And I have the option to pay the interest or not every year. I have chosen to pay the interest, so sometimes we need to borrow to top that off. I tell everyone I was allowed to stay in my family home thanks to HomeEquity Bank.

HomeEquity Bank clients may recognize your name because you performed for the "Our Homes Are Everything" campaign during the pandemic. Tell us about your musical career.

I perform and teach, but it seems to be all online now. I have played places like the China Orient Express on the train, and Alaskan cruises and private parties around Toronto. I teach private lessons and people used to come to my home, but now it's all via webcam, obviously. My website is online at www.johnagiusmusic.com, and I created a free album of meditation music called *The Healing Touch* for visitors to download there, to help people relax in these stressful times.

Boomers Today

Boomers today make up a huge part of our senior population. By July 2019, Canadians over 65 accounted for 17.5 percent of Canadians, whereas children aged 0 to 14 comprised only 16 percent. This is a reversal of past demographic norms. In 2020, even boomers born at the late end of the group, in 1965, are turning 55. By 2031, all boomers will have turned 65.

But boomers also stand out as a generation for other reasons. For one thing, boomer women joined the workforce in unprecedented numbers. Today's boomers are also fitter and more health-conscious than past generations. Even the older pre-boomer generation is very much engaged in the world. I see my own parents, who live in Poland, as a prime example of such seniors. They are excellent role models: They enjoyed good careers, and in retirement they have found ways to continue working, but not full time. They have friends and parties, dinners out, patio drinks and little weekend getaways. In 2019, they threw themselves a big celebration for their 50th wedding anniversary!

Parents on the move! Yvonne Ziomecki's parents, Lucy and Zbigniew Glogowski, in Amsterdam.

Every year as they get older, my parents have adjusted their pace, but they're still up for living their lives as they always have. For example, they have always travelled and, now in their seventies, they are still at it. In 2019, they went on a dream trip to China, and they are usually off somewhere, including Thailand and Cambodia and all over Europe. They loved Portugal, Barcelona, Amsterdam and St. Petersburg. They inspired me to do much of the travel that I've done. And apparently, they fit right in with their age group: according to a 2017 study by Expedia Group and Northstar Research, baby boomers travel the most of any current generation, at 28 days a year and with a preference for international destinations.

Travel is just one thing that typifies what I see as my parents', and indeed many of my clients', "younger attitude." Their brains are still engaged. They read a lot, keep up on current events, still have a sense of humour and can laugh at themselves. My dad always has the latest smartphone. Both my mother and father are always full of life advice. They're aging, but they're not letting their age define them. I love that attitude, and I think they've passed it on to me.

HomeEquity Bank's recent studies on aging confirm that most older people don't even see themselves as older. A 2018 Ipsos survey showed that the majority of Canadians 55 and older report that age stereotypes are totally out of line with how they see themselves. Nearly 80 percent don't even want to be called "seniors." Our follow-up study, in partnership with neuroscience research firm Brainsights and our creative agency Zulu Alpha Kilo, showed that boomers prefer ads that avoid labels and portray the demographic in a positive way. "Age-based identities are created and reinforced by society and through media and marketing that set expectations for how people should behave and conform," said Kevin Keane, Founder and CEO of Brainsights, when the study was released. "But 55+ audiences don't see themselves as old and frail. They're wise and energetic, with a passion for teaching, legacy and life fulfilment."

Yet, unfortunately, a more recent July 2020 survey on ageism by the National Poll on Healthy Aging at the University of Michigan confirmed that 82 percent of older adults experienced one or more form of everyday ageism in their daily lives, including ageist messages, ageism in interpersonal interactions and even internalized ageism. This needs to end. As Chris Farrell, author of *Unretirement: How Baby Boomers Are Changing the Way We Think About Work, Community, and the Good Life* puts it in his preface to the book, after naming off all of the reasons why America has come to fear the aging of the boomer generation, from the loss of workplace expertise to the absorption of health care resources, this age group is something to celebrate. "The dire jeremiads aimed at an aging America are wrong and deeply mis-placed," writes Farrell. "The graying of America is terrific news. Living longer is good. Embrace the realization that boomers on average are healthier and better educated than previous genera-tions. An aging population presents an enormous opportunity for society and for aging individuals to seize and exploit."

While we've been providing a picture of the boomer set, and while all boomers now qualify as clients (given that even the youngest among them are now 55), our clients, of course, include pre-boomers as well. As children of the Great Depression, parents of boomers are generally noted to be born between 1901 and 1945. They are sometimes characterized as the traditionalists that boomers pushed back against. While boomers saw prosperity, the pre-boomer generation witnessed the nearly 30 percent unemployment rate that Canada experienced during the Depression era.

Happy HomeEquity Bank client Brigitte V.

Given the diversity of Canada's older population, this may be a good moment to note that it's challenging to lump all people 55 and older into a single category because they are at different stages of aging. Sociologists refer to the subcategories of aging as young-old (65–74), middle-old (75–84) and old-old (over 85), noting that there's a diversity of experiences among these groups, with physical and cognitive limitations often increasing with age. If you've met people in each of these ranges, you know all this without having to hear it from a sociologist.

As for the boomers, today's young-old group is much more active than such folks were in the past, and further away from the average age of death and decline. And they are also at a point where they still can and are preparing for the later age stages—something that's evident in actions like postponing retirement to boost their nest egg even further or making long-term decisions about how and where they will live. As they consider options for their future aging, perhaps the reverse mortgage will fit in to some people's plans.

MEET THE TEAM: ROLAND MACKINTOSH, DISTRICT VICE PRESIDENT, WEST TORONTO

One of the secrets to HomeEquity Bank's success is our caring team! We've sprinkled a handful of Q&As with team members throughout the book to help share even more client stories and perspectives.

What's your background?

I've been with HomeEquity Bank since 2002!

Who are some of your most memorable clients?

I had a client, a woman about 70 years old, we connected through her bank. She had reunited with her brother through the website Ancestry.com. They had been separated during the Second World War when the bombs were going off in the UK, and she hadn't seen him in 40 years. And she couldn't qualify for a line of credit from the bank, but she had a house worth $850,000. We approved her for $200,000 within a week. She was over the moon. The first thing she did was book a flight to London, caught up with her brother. And then two things happened: She started to go back and forth, because he had a little place in Malta and they became best pals. But within three years, she actually ended up selling her house in Oakville and moving to the UK, because she got hitched! She met a man there and they ended up getting married.

Another client was a gentleman in Watertown, Ontario, just west of Toronto. This is a life-saving story. This gentleman was 80 years old, on dialysis. When he was about 70 years old, another bank had approved him for mortgage. He was doing what's called a spousal buyout because of a marital breakdown. We call this "grey divorce," very prominent right now in Canada. When COVID-19 happened, the rental income he had stopped coming in and he went back to the bank pleading for some kind of relief, a mortgage deferral payment. It got so bad that he told me that for the last three days of every single month, he was eating canned soup for breakfast, lunch and dinner. He was out of money. And he didn't want to risk defaulting on his house that he fought so hard to gain control over.

We did the deal within one week. I fast-tracked this guy's application because I heard he was not eating properly. We put $100,000 extra in his bank account. And I asked him, what are you going to do now? And he was so happy. Gave me a hug. Said he's going to have a steak dinner for the first time in five years. He told me he was so worried that on his deathbed, he'd have his family thinking he's a failure. And he said, "You have given me the gift of peace of mind."

What do you like about working for HomeEquity Bank?

People ask why I've been in this business for 18 years with the same bank. It's because we truly help people. We've seen clients with million-dollar homes in Oakville with no mortgage but $60,000 in credit card debt. And the worry and the stress they've been going through, and finally they feel like they can ask someone for help. And the traditional bank says, "You don't have the income to support a line of credit on your house, even though it's free and clear. And I know it sucks having $60,000 for the credit card debts, but would you like to have a glass of water?" And you know, that's the kind of treatment they've been getting. HomeEquity Bank is different.

CHAPTER FOUR

THE JOY OF AGING IN PLACE

For all of us at HomeEquity Bank, our daily inspiration for aging in place at its best comes from our clients. By choosing a CHIP Reverse Mortgage, they're taking action to liquidate the money they need from their houses. Rather than rushing to any of the more precarious or hasty alternatives like lines of credit or downsizing (we'll discuss those in another chapter), our clients are seizing control to make aging in place a reality. They're taking action to keep their house while still accomplishing their goals, whether it be to improve their financial situation or improve their living space in preparation for longer-term needs. They're using the reverse mortgage for a renovation that will make their home safer in retirement or liquidating some cash to build up their reserves for services like lawn care or snow removal. They're being proactive in exploring whether the reverse mortgage will be the right way to support their aging-in-place plan.

We're inspired by people like Deanna W., who realized that the reverse mortgage would be a good option to get her in-laws out of debt. Or Angelo Abbate, who took action to ease his debt load, so he didn't have to work so much in his seventies. Each of these clients were looking for a level-headed solution and found it in the reverse mortgage, and now both are breathing easier. We now think of them as models for aging in place, because they sought out the resources they required to do just that.

But what does "aging in place" mean? The Canadian government ministry responsible for seniors defines aging in place as "having the health and social support and services you need to live safely and independently in your home or your community for as long as you wish and are able." The ministry also provides some questions to help Canadians think realistically about how they will do that, including considering what modifications they might need to make to their homes (for example, installing hand rails or ramps) in order to remain safe; reflecting on how they will maintain their home if they need help; and researching what support services, from social to community to financial services, might be available that they can look into now.

Other resources are available as well that focus specifically on helping people to plan their aging in place. Aginginplace.org provides some useful links, and Virginia Morris's How to Care for Aging Parents offers a guide for adult children. Perhaps one of the best is How to Age in Place: Planning for a Happy, Independent, and Financially Secure Retirement by Mary A. Languirand and Robert F. Bornstein. This book is divided into two sections. The first is called "Making It Work" and it focuses on practical matters from funding your retirement to assessing the accessibility of your home and neighbourhood, and the second is called "Making It Count," which focuses on discovering purpose and meaning in later life.

In their Introduction, Languirand and Bornstein share a checklist of factors that readers must consider when making plans to age in place. These factors include financial planning; safe housing; neighbourhood safety and walkability; accessibility of services (for example, pharmacy and grocery); proactive medical and mental health care; opportunities for community, cultural and civic engagement; and sustainability. In their epilogue, the authors remind the reader

Happy HomeEquity Bank clients Gordon and Audrey A.

that "retirement is not just a time to look back and reminisce, but it's also an opportunity to look forward, set new goals and make choices about the person you want to become."

So, there are resources out there for those who want to age in place. And there is definitely the desire to do so. A recent National Institute of Ageing/Telus Health survey reports that "100 percent of Canadians 65 years of age and older who report that they intend to do whatever they can to stay active and maintain optimal health and independence plan on supporting themselves to live safely and independently in their own home as long as possible."

Our own survey showed that seven out of 10 say they want to maintain a sense of independence during their retirement years, and of those over 75, half say they want to stay close to family. Forty percent say emotional attachment to the home and neighbourhood are also a substantial part of their lives. So, the evidence clearly shows how desirable aging in place is for older Canadians. What there is less of is planning how to make that happen—really taking a look at both finances and living space, planning out scenarios for the future and seeing what kind of supports are needed and available.

For many people who are just crossing the threshold into our client base of 55 and older (welcome!), investigating the reverse mortgage as an option is about reckoning with your plans for your future and realizing it could be a lengthy future. The fact is, people are living longer: In 1920, the life expectancy at birth for Canadian men was 58.8 years and for women it was 60.6 years. Today it is 80 and 84, respectively. For a Canadian woman retiring at age 65, that's a full 20 future years to prepare for. And that's just the average! Canada now boasts quite the cohort of centenarians, too—well over eleven thousand. How exciting to think that people reading this book may also live into three digits! But it's definitely more exhilarating to think about being a hundred when you've planned for that possibility than when you haven't.

CLIENT SPOTLIGHT: ANGELO ABBATE

We've sprinkled a handful of Q&As with inspirational clients through-out the book to provide a sampling of the real voices behind people who have chosen the reverse mortgage.

What was your financial situation before you got a reverse mortgage?

I was in a lot of trouble financially for the last two years. In 2018, I had a heart attack and had to have a quadruple bypass. That put me out of commission for four months. In my business, in automobile sales, that four months of income could relate to anywhere from $20,000 to $30,000. So, that put us back financially. My wife still works, too. She's in the daycare business.

So, we ended up taking out a loan to try and recover. That was stupid because it was like 20-something percent interest. I got behind on a lot of payments. I came back to work in January 2019, and a couple of months later I started feeling ill. I was diagnosed as a possible type 2 diabetic, which was unusual for my age. At that point, I was 70. I got sicker, and I lost weight. They did more tests and said, "There's something in your stomach. We think it's cancer."

So, a lot of things happened. I could barely work. I was dealing with Sunnybrook Hospital, the cancer wing, and St. Michael's Hospital. So, that dragged on through the winter—another four-and-a-half months that I couldn't work. I collected a little bit of EI, and here we go back into the whole second mortgage. My credit cards were maxed up to almost $20,000. Everybody was calling me. I was avoiding calls, avoiding people. I just was struggling.

How did you connect with HomeEquity Bank?

An angel walked into my life. Mortgage Specialist Krista Zingel came to my dealership. She was looking to buy a small used SUV. We got talking, sitting at my desk. This all happened just before the pandemic shutdown. I'm a talker, and she is, too. So, we're sitting there talking about cars. And Krista looked at me and she said, "You don't look quite right." And I said, "I'm not feeling great either." I told her about being sick and everything. And she asked me if I owned my house and how old I was and how old my wife was. And she whipped out her business card and said, "I think maybe I can help you." I went home that night and started talking to my wife. We invited Krista to the house. She met with my wife and my two kids, who are both adults but still living at home. She explained it very, very well. We saw the benefits. And we went from there.

My wife was as excited as I was when we understood that all our debts would be cleared and that we could start from scratch. And even though my credit at that point was terrible, Krista said it's not based on your credit. It has to do with the equity in your house.

What has it meant to you to get a CHIP Reverse Mortgage, and do you have plans for the money, beyond debt repayment?

It was such a huge relief. My wife and I are at the point now where we have the end of the month, $4,000 to $5,000 in our chequing account, which we haven't had for many, many years—and that's with all the bills paid by the end of the month. I'm also getting my credit score back up slowly. It's going to take a while. But you know what? We don't need anything. We're still doing a few things around the house. Our garage door is literally almost falling apart. Last year, I would have sweated it and said, "How can I patch this to last one more winter?" Such a relief. The other thing, too, is now I can sleep. I was really struggling. I was stressed. I was making myself sick.

A DARKER PICTURE

While we're inspired when our clients take action to improve their finances, we have to admit we're sometimes worried by some of the situations people are in when they first come to see us. Sometimes, prospective clients are anxious and in crisis. They're also looking for a solution, but maybe they've waited and worried too long. Sometimes the place they are coming from is dark. It brings to mind this quote by playwright Tennessee Williams: "You can be young without money, but you can't be old without it."

Like it or not, aging is easier with money, and we meet many people whose dire financial circumstances mean that they are not living their best life in retirement. These cash flow crunches happen for so many reasons. Maybe someone made a bad investment. Maybe the roof leaked. Maybe the person is not great with budgeting and it turns out that there are more expenses than they anticipated in retirement. And no wonder, as property taxes or insurance premiums or hydro bills are always on the rise, not to mention the cost of groceries. It's difficult to estimate the rising costs of living decades before they happen.

Whatever the reasons for cash flow problems, it's a major stressor. And often when people call us at HomeEquity Bank, they may have waited so long that things have gotten worse in the interim, or they may have already gone down the more expensive path of a second mortgage at a high interest rate. All the while, they wonder how they will pay off the growing minimum payment each month, not to mention the principal and the hefty fees.

And they get themselves into more debt. Sadly, there's a lot of shame around this—people feel like they have failed or haven't made the right life decisions. And like everyone, they compare themselves to others and decide that they don't measure up.

An example comes to mind about a client who recently came to us only when she had maxed out both her line of credit of almost $50,000 and a credit card with a limit of $10,000. Those come with high interest rates, especially the credit card! But she only has a limited pension income, under $1,000 per month, so you can understand how it would be hard to stick to that. More and more expenses ended up on this client's credit card, and that pressure really made her feel trapped. By the time she called us, she had only $4,000 left on one credit card to access. All the while, she lives in a home worth over $600,000! When she found out that she was eligible for a CHIP Reverse Mortgage, she was so relieved. She told us she could finally sleep at night. Her life changed for the better.

At HomeEquity Bank, we all believe that people in retirement deserve to be proud and feel empowered, not stressed and ashamed. Financial guru Suze Orman addresses this worry in the first chapter of her book *The Ultimate Retirement Guide for 50+: Winning Strategies to Make Your Money Last a Lifetime*. Noting that a good spirit is the among the best equipment you can have when tackling your finances, Orman writes, "Stop focusing on what you didn't do or could have done differently. Stop beating yourself up about how you should have more, or how you should be in control of your finances at this point in your life. Stop being paralyzed by the fear of what may happen years from now." Powerful message, isn't it?

We've met people who are too afraid to tell their kids they are worried about money. Sometimes it's not even that they are in crisis, but that things they once enjoyed before retirement suddenly seem to be a luxury and it's hard to give them up. They miss going out for dinner a couple of times a month. Or taking a winter holiday. Sometimes inertia plays a big part and they've just resigned themselves to living a very restricted life for years, budgeting line by line to avoid admitting that life would be more comfortable with a bit of a cushion. Having these limitations at this age is so frustrating.

Sometimes when cash-strapped people finally start to consider a reverse mortgage, they have been stuck feeling like they've been living with no options for a while. They will connect with our call centre and it will be the first time they've ever voiced their financial concerns. Often, it's a real release for them to share what's been troubling them. The sad thing is that while people are entangled in the trauma of debt, they're going about their daily lives, worrying about their financial problems, residing inside their most profitable investment. That house could be doing so much more for them! Everyone at our company always reminds potential clients, especially when we hear them down on themselves, that they did make at least one very smart decision—they bought a house!

CLIENT SPOTLIGHT:
THE CHUNG FAMILY (DEANNA W.)

We've sprinkled a handful of Q&As with inspirational clients through-out the book to provide a sampling of the real voices behind people who have chosen the reverse mortgage.

How did you learn about the reverse mortgage and realize it could help your family?

I'd seen some commercials on TV and then I did some research on the internet to see what was available in Canada. I was looking for mortgages for seniors, and HomeEquity Bank came up.

I'm the daughter-in-law. My husband's family had significant debts because of some legal problems. They are Korean, so they don't speak English or French. And other family members are not well-versed in mortgages, home equities. So, I'm the go-between. Their house was in jeopardy of being taken by the bank. They had to solve the debt problem and they couldn't go to a traditional bank. We had done some work with private lenders for 10 years, but that's exorbitant. That just wasn't a possibility. I'm sorry that I didn't think of CHIP sooner.

I was looking for a second mortgage and found out that HomeEquity Bank could help us. The broker I was matched up with was very confident from the beginning that we could cover the debt with HomeEquity Bank. He said, "Don't worry, I can help get you a reverse mortgage, it will be a lot more manageable." We arranged this all during the start of the coronavirus pandemic.

What does your family plan to do with the money?

We wanted to pay off the conventional mortgage and also make some improvements to the house. They need a new door, and we'd like to put some things in to make it easier for my mother-in-law to get around—handlebars and things.

What's their house like?

My in-laws live in a triplex. It's just outside the city centre. We live near Montreal. Their house has a nice little backyard, so they have their own little garden retreat, sitting in the backyard under an umbrella. There's enough space for a little garden. It's very close to the highway and the hospital. We're quite accessible to the city, but it's a quiet area, with a nice park across the street, skating in the winter, a baseball diamond where you can watch the kids play baseball in the summer, and park benches. It's a great location, within walking distance to a grocery store.

How does your family spend time together?

My mother-in-law is 78 and my father-in-law is 80. They're in decent health. My mother-in-law has some mobility issues and she doesn't drive. I've been married to my partner for about 11 years. We live five minutes away. We go over and visit a lot. We do a lot of shopping and just bringing things over and visiting. There's nothing like Mom's cooking—she makes traditional Korean food and so do we, so we'll cook and exchange. We help out, like when they're not able to get out in the car in the winter. Or during the pandemic, we did their shopping for them. We bring things over because it's not as easy for them to get out as often.

What has it meant to you to get a reverse mortgage?

I was absolutely relieved to get the reverse mortgage. Before, they were paying $3,500 a month! It was a high interest rate, something ridiculous like 15 percent, so going to 5 percent was great.

TURNING YOUR HOME INTO SECURITY

So, one reason that many people start looking into a reverse mortgage is to get some extra cash flow. It may be for a big emergency expense, but often it is also the need for regular small expenses that have just added up. While our clients made the super-smart investment of buying a house (and keeping it in good condition by investing further in upkeep), sometimes they don't have a savings cushion or maybe just not a big enough one for the kinds of expenses that come up these days. As we explored in Chapter One, pensions are in fast decline. With today's trend towards gig and contract employment, it may get even worse in the future. There are other groups that never had pensions to begin with: people who work in the arts or small business owners, for example. Or sometimes a business owner plans to sell it for their retirement cushion and then something goes wrong, such as the pandemic. Who could have predicted that? Unfortunately, then the business goes into decline, through no fault of their own, and there's no money to survive a prolonged closure.

Many people don't even think about retirement planning until it's late in the game. A 2018 CIBC poll showed that 90 percent of Canadians don't have a formal and detailed retirement plan, and 53 percent aren't sure they are saving enough. If you consider when boomers were born, the average life expectancy was 63 years of age. Today we need to do more planning for longer and more active retirements.

By the time many of our clients call HomeEquity Bank, they're at the point where they've started to realize they had been overly optimistic about what they would spend in retirement. Or they figured beforehand that they would just live on less. But then when they actually reach retirement, they find it's harder than they thought. Who wants to be scrimping in what we used to think of as golden years? By the time these folks come to us, they are tired of constantly having to record absolutely every expense. They just want more of a buffer.

A DIFFERENT WAY TO LOOK AT YOUR HOUSE

One reason people may not have saved as much is because they figured they could count on their house as another source of funding for their retirement. But let's face it, it's not until retirement that we truly think about how to turn the house into a money maker. Prior to then, our options may have included downsizing or a home equity line of credit that not everyone realizes can be hard to qualify for in older age. The choice of credit cards to pay for essentials can be a slippery slope, even in the short term, due to their high interest rates. We'll discuss some of these other options further in the next chapter.

If it wasn't for the CHIP Reverse Mortgage, I would not have a home anymore.
- Margaret

Rated on ★ Trustpilot

HomeEquity Bank

It's not that people aren't thinking about their house as a great source of equity, but when they're younger they always figure, "If anything ever gets too desperate, we can always just sell the house and move into a smaller place." When you're younger, maybe you *do* feel that way—like moving is an adventure or you want to try new living arrangements. But the temptation to try new things doesn't stay with us. And we are also looking with rose-coloured glasses before it comes time to act. Idly thinking you'll sell your house someday is quite different than facing the actual inconvenience of moving.

Again, that's like thinking, *I'll just tighten my belt at retirement*, but when it comes time to do that, you realize it's not such a fun option. Moving is a lot of work, and it's not as if you can just sell a piece of your house. Also, there's a certain amount of shame attached to the realization that you haven't saved enough. People think that they made a mistake with their budget and so they just have to live with it. Sadly, they rationalize that they will just make do. When people get into this cycle, they start to view everything as a luxury. Inertia sets in and they look at everything as nice-to-haves and try to keep reminding themselves that they're lucky just to be able to live within their means.

Or they rationalize that something is a want rather than a need. But what's wrong with aspiring to fulfill your wants? Wanting to complete that kitchen or bathroom renovation? Wanting to go on a winter holiday every other year? These are not huge luxuries. Sometimes they are even necessary for safety, like the bathroom renovation that could prevent a fall. There isn't really a safety aspect to the winter holiday, but there is a huge mental health reward in taking a vacation, and that's not to be taken as lightly as we sometimes do.

And yet what our clients also have in common is the relief that at least they have a house they can live in. And it seems like the more you age, the more you realize how much you just love your house! You've spent years renovating to make it just the way you like it. You've grown to really love your neighbourhood and local community. So, this is the other option we're trying to make people see—that they can still view their house as a source of money, but in a different way. Homeowners have this amazing investment and a real estate market that's been on fire for the past two decades. The challenge is just to liquidate it, and we have the solution.

These are the financial worries we see from older adults—but that's before they become clients. Because when they finally come to see us, there's a transformation. First, even just by calling to find out what's possible with the reverse mortgage, people have moved out of inertia into action. Then when they take it up, their world opens up to possibility. All those modest things that were thought of as nice-to-haves (but are really more than that) become within their means. When you've already made this amazing investment in a house, why wouldn't you get that investment to work harder for you and fund the life you actually want, instead of feeling jealous of other people? That lifestyle is within your reach. Or even just the calm that comes from not having to pinch every penny. It's so freeing.

EXPERT SPOTLIGHT: DR. SAMIR SINHA: GERIATRICIAN, AGING ADVOCATE AND SILVER FOX WHISPERER

Sitting down to interview Dr. Sinha about his perspective on aging was an invaluable experience. In Chapter One, we shared some of his knowledge about public health measures as they relate to the aging population, including the inspiration we might take from other countries and what's possible from a societal perspective. In this second part of our interview, we tap into Dr. Sinha's wisdom and experience as a medical doctor to get some tips on what older people can do to ensure they age in place successfully.

What attracted you to the field of geriatrics? And what exactly does a geriatrician do?

Did you know that the *New York Times* has called geriatricians "a rare and endangered species?" While our population is aging faster than ever before, my specialty only came into medicine in the 1980s in Canada. So, we actually have an odd situation where we have 10 times as many pediatricians in our country as we do geriatricians. For me, I've always been interested in working with vulnerable populations. I don't want anybody to ever think that older adults are helpless individuals. They are a population that has made huge contributions to our society. And yet, they have to make do with a health care system that was designed for a younger population. And a society obsessed with staying younger.

As a geriatrician, I care for the whole patient. I'm seen as an expert in complexity. My job is often to play the quarterback, to understand the whole patient with her team of doctors and to try to get everything coordinated and organized. The majority of my patients tend to be frail, older. Sometimes I see them in crisis. Sometimes I see them pre-crisis. I see them in hospital, for home visits, in clinic and by telemedicine. Often, they're on multiple medications. They're having trouble with their physical functioning and their cognitive functioning.

What advice would you have for older people want to stay healthy while aging in place?

I do have a subset of patients, approximately 10 percent, who see me because they are trying to stay healthy and retain their independence in their communities for as long as possible. They want to be proactive. I call these my "silver foxes." Some of them are even in their late nineties, doing incredibly well! And they want to keep it that way. So, I encourage them! I always say a good offence is a great defence.

There's a lot of really strong evidence about things we can do to stay healthy and independent. There are studies that show that about 30 percent of dementias are actually preventable. For example, they've found that if you completed high school, you're less likely to end up with dementia, because you've exercised your brain at a young age and you've actually made it stronger and more resilient as a result. Treating things like hearing loss early on is another example that can help. If you actually start dealing with these things more proactively at a younger age, stopping hearing loss can help protect your brain and reduce the risk that you might develop dementia.

Are there also lifestyle factors to consider?

Definitely. If you smoke, for example, you increase the risk of developing heart disease or vascular disease, which can lead to strokes and heart attacks, which in turn can affect your memory. Eating a reasonably balanced diet and drinking within moderation are helpful. Exercising regularly—for all ages we recommend about 150 minutes a week. Going for a brisk walk, something that makes you huff and puff a little. That type of exercise that is going to help protect your brain and keep you strong and fit.

Sometimes my silver foxes come into my office with a whole boat-load of vitamins and minerals. I tell them, if you're eating a well-balanced diet, you don't need all of that stuff. But do make sure your thyroid is in check and your vitamin B_{12} level is where it should be. Basically, you can handle all of these checks with a good primary care provider who is being proactive and doing things like making sure you get appropriate cancer screenings. Make sure that you're screened for any heart issues.

Any other things that your average senior might not think of?

Another thing is vaccines! There's a vaccine we recommend for all older adults called the pneumococcal vaccine, and children get it, too. But if 95 percent of children under two years of age get that shot, what is the percentage of those over 65 you would imagine get it? Only 40 percent!

Everybody knows that kids get vaccinations, but we forget that older adults need vaccinations too. When the silver foxes come and see me, I always ask if they're getting their annual influenza vaccinations. I check up on the pneumonia vaccine, shingles, and ask if they get a tetanus shot every 10 years. Just like the pediatric vaccination schedule, there is a vaccination schedule for older adults as well.

How can an aspiring silver fox get started navigating their old age?

I always ask my silver foxes to think down the road—what are ways that they can make their lives and their homes easier in case they do become more functionally limited? What equipment can you buy, what services can you arrange now like, say, grocery delivery, to support you to remain healthy and independent in your home as long as possible? How can you make your house safer to prevent yourself from falling?

It's hard to adjust when you're in crisis, so why not think about it now?

When I meet a patient for the first time, I always ask them what matters most to them and what's important to them. I've never had a patient who said, "I aspire to end up in a nursing home forever," right? Okay, I had one, but she was like, a hundred. Most people tell me they want to stay healthy and independent in their own home. So, I tell them, if that's what you want, what would that look like for you?

Most people have not really had those conversations. I think it's like we don't want to think about the future or our eventual death. I talk to families about whether they've assigned powers of attorney or made an advanced care plan. Sometimes it helps people be a bit more proactive and realize that they have to make sure they're eating well, doing other healthy things. And if they have a limited budget, then it helps them to get real—okay, how do how do we spend it? Or when do we spend it? To maximize your time to age in place.

Why don't more people know about how to prepare for aging? Any more tips?

Most people have never navigated aging. They don't really know what is possible and what can be done. But there are several things that people can do to stay at home. There are government-funded home-care services and traditional home-care services that may be useful. Many of my patients are not aware of them or that they exist across many provinces and territories. There are also community support services agencies, organizing things from local transportation services specifically designed for older adults, to services like Meals on Wheels.

It's about understanding what are their issues? What's making it harder for them to stay healthy and independent? Sometimes it's just the medical issues that need to be sorted, and the person is back to being healthy and independent in their community. I have lots of patients who've been in those situations, where you just fix some things that were broken, and they've got a new lease on life.

When people arrive in crisis, by then they're now utilizing a lot of services, not a little. And that little service that we could have started you on proactively could have prevented that big fall. And that hospitalization that now will only allow you to go home if you can find 24-hour care, which the government doesn't provide, except for nursing homes, is very expensive.

What about mental health?

There are also community services to help combat loneliness and social isolation. Social isolation doesn't equal loneliness: a lot of people like to be on their own. But there are other people who don't like to be socially isolated and it can trigger depression, anxiety and other mental health issues. Studies show that loneliness itself can increase your risk of dying by 45 percent. Also, one in four older Canadians tells us they don't have a family member or friend close at hand who could help them with getting a basic task completed, like filling a prescription or getting groceries. This is a real concern.

In Ontario, we have over three hundred of what we call Seniors Active Living Centres, where hundreds of thousands of older adults hang out every year. These are amazing opportunities for people to continue to rebuild their social connections, as they may have withered out as people lose loved ones and friends. There are similar centres across the country.

How can we make a better environment for aging in our communities?

There's a movement that started just over a decade ago, the World Health Organization's Global Network for Age-friendly Cities and Communities. It's based on rethinking the physical spaces that we negotiate, like our transit systems, our neighbourhoods and our communities. For older adults who can no longer drive, it's still important to get around. Once you lose your ability to drive, you're pretty much trapped and a prisoner in your own home. Over time, we're seeing more Canadian cities and communities moving towards becoming these age-friendly communities. I'm the co-chair of the City of Toronto's Seniors Strategy, and I've helped Toronto become Canada's largest city that has been designated by the World Health Organization as an age-friendly city.

As an example, we've now installed park benches that have little arms on the chairs to help older people get in and out more easily. We've also increased the number, placing thousands more benches in areas where seniors are likely to gather, like seniors' residences or in neighbourhoods where there is a higher concentration of older adults. Another thing we've done is to delay street-crossing times in those areas. So older, tired legs have a few extra seconds to make it across the street safely, rather than trying to run the 50-yard dash and risk falling and fracturing a hip. Small changes like these allow for more of a city's oldest citizens to remain healthy and independent in their own community.

CHAPTER FIVE

WHY REVERSE MORTGAGES OUTSHINE THE ALTERNATIVES

We mentioned in the last chapter that there are so many conflicting emotions around debt and retirement. In the personal finance blog *The Simple Dollar*, Kristen Kuchar writes about the emotional effect of debt, noting that it's about more than money and can lead to psychological issues including depression and anxiety, resentment, denial, stress, anger, frustration, regret, shame and fear. By contrast, paying off debt can lead to relief, freedom and accomplishment. We have seen all these emotions expressed by our clients.

We also hear a lot of about there being mixed emotions about the reverse mortgage product, unfortunately. Certain rumours still abound regarding the product, which stop people from even looking into it. Sometimes these misconceptions come from practices in other countries, and sometimes they are based on old information. One of the most persistent misconceptions is that people still think they can lose their house by using a reverse mortgage. Not with us. You always maintain title ownership and control of your home. We deliberately lend conservatively to a maximum of 55 percent (and at a smaller percentage to many of our younger borrowers), so that even if the housing market does a total reversal of the past decades and stops appreciating, a borrower will still have enough money in the home to cover the reverse mortgage. This is our "No Negative Equity Guarantee."

Even bankers can be misinformed, not realizing that our product can help many older clients. Thankfully, all that's changing, as we keep reaching out to bankers and brokers and educating them about our product. Given that the older demographic is not always a bank's highest priority, they are often happy to be able to connect clients with us, and we even work together to help clients. As a bank, we are getting more and more referrals from both bankers and brokers. But it's frustrating to have a product that can help so many more than it is helping, and to realize that it's not coming to mind with the same frequency as other alternatives.

While of course we are big proponents of the reverse mortgage, even we will admit that it may not be right for everyone. For someone who has so much debt that they are really struggling with their financial obligations, it may indeed make more sense to sell their home and downsize. Or for someone who is looking for an extremely short-term solution, for which they will have the money to pay back within a few months, the revolving nature of a home equity line of credit could make more sense if you qualify for it. But for many people, the reverse mortgage can work better than some of the options that traditionally come more quickly to mind.

CHIPReverseMortgage ⌂
by HomeEquity Bank

After retiring in 2004, Steve and Cindy considered downsizing to ensure they had the funds to live comfortably through retirement. Instead of selling their beloved home in Burnaby, BC when it was worth $325,000, they chose to take control with CHIP, and today own a house that is worth over **$1.6 Million.**

$325,000

$1,600,000+

2004

2019

Thanks to CHIP, they were able to get the money they needed for retirement without having to sell their home and they still have

$1,335,207

remaining in home equity.

In this chapter, we look at some other options, from downsizing to home equity lines of credit to even moving into a seniors' residence. We'll alert you to some of the factors you should consider when looking at each of them. This will help you to gain a clearer picture of these alternatives and consider the reverse mortgage alongside them. Let's start by looking at one of the most popular options: downsizing.

Downsizing

Downsizing is one of those far-off plans that sounds like a good idea when it's still somewhere off in the future. Like losing weight, when you think, *I'll lose weight sometime because I know it's good for my health.* But anyone who has tried to lose weight knows that once you vow to start, it's easier said than done! The same is true of downsizing.

In today's hot real estate market, some think that their shortcut to solving money problems, such as an underfunded retirement, is to cash in on their pot-of-gold house by moving elsewhere and putting the rest in the bank for a rainy day. Another possible influence may also be coming from minimalist trendsetter Marie Kondo, who has inspired us by suggesting that it's easy to clean up our decades of clutter by discarding anything that "does not give us joy."

Whatever their reasons, many people are confident that not only will they be happier in a smaller space, but they will make a huge profit on selling their house. And yes, it does work out that way for certain people. But we have also heard stories that are less triumphant. HomeEquity Bank commissioned a survey from Ipsos that found that 27 percent of downsizers found the costs were more than they expected. Often when they commit to the decision of downsizing, homeowners become so excited about the idea that they don't always think about all the costs involved. But add up realtor fees, lawyer fees at a few thousand, moving costs and possibly the cost of new furniture if, for instance, your big old couch from your house isn't exactly condo-sized or condo chic.

As an example, take the average 2019 Toronto home price of $819,319 (let's round it to $800,000 for ease of math). The cumulative costs of downsizing might add up to reduce the profit by $50,000. So, the profits could be less than you think. And that's not even counting the hassle factor of packing up your stuff (and sorting and tossing a portion if you're moving to a smaller place) and going through all the stress of dealing with real estate agents, negotiating in a hot real estate market and coordinating the actual move itself. Packing up your belongings and unpacking them is hard on the physical health of many older people.

But even more important than the financial and material tolls are the emotional factors, several of which we've already mentioned. Often people who move out of their homes don't realize that they may not be able to buy back into their former neighbourhoods, especially in fast-paced markets like Toronto and Vancouver. And a move may sound adventurous when you describe the fun of exploring a new community or making new friends, but we've met lots of people who tell us they miss their old neighbourhoods, from their familiar evening walk, to the favourite restaurant they used to go to on Saturdays, to the recreation centre down the street. Many older adults move out to smaller centres without realizing they've also moved away from hospitals or their familiar family doctors.

People also tell us they miss their long-time neighbours, the good folks they used to have over for drinks or chatted with when doing yard work. And it turns out, it's not as easy to make friends as an adult, especially when you're an older adult and you no longer have kids to bring you together as parents. These things seem minor until you discover they are not.

Even more serious is the emotional impact of the actual house you're giving up. For many, it's the place where they raised a family. There are so many memories there, of birthdays or weekend movie nights or hosting family get-togethers. People may act like these are just a moment in time or tell themselves that they will make more memories, but it takes time for a new place to become a memory-filled home.

We've talked to people who have made the move to downsize, believing that they will love the downtown urban life in a chic condo only to tell us they miss their house in the suburbs. Or people who move out to the country and miss their local coffee shop and urban yoga studio more than they expected. Yes, you may vow to make an effort to drive into town to make use of your symphony subscription, but will you? In reality, it's harder to manage when the commute is an hour away and you're getting older. Especially in winter!

One person who thought downtown city life would be the life for her is Joyce Wayne, who has intrepidly documented her own misadventures in downsizing as the author of HomeEquity

Bank's "Retirement Matters" blog (www.chip.ca/reverse-mort-gage-resources/joyce-wayne-retirement-matters/). She wrote about the ordeal of moving from Oakville to Toronto and back again in her blog series for the *Globe and Mail*, and we asked her to recall that journey here in this chapter. (Spoiler alert: It all worked out. She's happier than ever.)

THE DOWNSIZING DILEMMA: A TALE BOTH CAUTIONARY AND JOYFUL

by Joyce Wayne

"Retirement Matters" blogger Joyce Wayne. (Shan Qiao Photography)

Once my daughter began applying for university, I decided that I no longer needed the spacious home in Oakville I'd owned for almost 20 years. It wasn't that I didn't enjoy my quiet, tree-lined neighbourhood. It was more that I was itching for new beginnings—or longing to revisit old ones. I'd been a single mother for the last many years, and I was intent on returning to the downtown Toronto district of Queen Street West, where I'd launched my career as a journalist.

On a beautiful fall day, I drove past an imposing billboard for this new condominium, the "Bohemian Embassy." Upon entering the sales office, an extremely pleasant salesperson gave me a tour of the mock-ups and pictures of the suites. Within hours, I'd chosen one that included a massive terrace with views of the city and the lake, two bedrooms and a party room on the top floor for entertaining. That same week, I borrowed from the line of credit on my Oakville home to secure a down payment on the condo. Six years later, when the condo was finally ready for me to move in, another new condo blocked my view of Lake Ontario and the CN Tower. A year later, my view of the city was blocked by yet another new high-rise erected so close to my balcony that I could see the tenant's television screen across the lane.

After two years as a resident of my condo, I was ready to return to living in a house—a structure with its own entrance, its own back garden, its own driveway, and neighbours who were mature and responsible enough to avoid playing music at 3 a.m. and flicking cigarette butts that burned holes in my balcony furniture. Between the aggravation of the fire alarm going off all hours of the day and night, the rising condo fees and the 850-square-foot apartment where entertaining friends and family was next to impossible, I gave up on condo living. Instead, I listed my unit for sale and purchased a townhouse in my home city of Oakville, a stone's throw from Lake Ontario. Now I revel in the fact that I can sit on my deck drinking a cocktail at sundown, barbequing a steak—dog by my side—without cigarette butts falling on my head.

The only issue was, it was harder than ever by 2013 to get back into a home in the Greater Toronto Area. My accountant tells me that many of her clients wish to return to homes in Oakville after moving away—to condos or to the country—but house prices keep rising. After realtor and legal fees, moving costs and furnishing my new home, I was forced to negotiate a mortgage for the townhouse. I'm still paying the mortgage down every month. It's getting smaller, but my gamble with downsizing and condo living cost me more than I ever expected.

Joyce Wayne is HomeEquity Bank's "Retirement Matters" blogger. She first documented her downsizing journey in a blog series for the Globe and Mail.

The downside
of downsizing

Fees	Downsizing	CHIP Reverse Mortgage
Real Estate Fees (Average 5% of selling price)	FOR SALE $40,000	N/A
Legal Fees (Sale and purchase)	$2,500	$500-$900
Land Transfer Tax (Varies depending on province and city)	$0-$16,950	N/A
Moving Expenses (Movers, boxes, garbage removal, etc)	$3,000	N/A
Furnishing & Upgrades	$5,000	N/A
Condo Fees ($300 - $1,200 per month)	$3,600-$14,400	N/A
Home Appraisal	$300-$500	$300-$600
Administration Fee	N/A	$1,795-$1,995
Total	**$54,400 - $82,350**	**$2,595 - $3,495**

HomeEquity Bank

Condos and Rentals

For many older adults who decide to downsize, it's into a condo. In these cases, they aren't always prepared for the rules involved, from the monthly commitment of rising condo fees to the rules around plants, pets and noise. We've heard from people who say they miss not only the size of their house, but also things they didn't plan on missing, like washing their car in the driveway, gardening in a real flowerbed or inviting friends to sit out in the privacy of their shaded porch.

The same challenges apply when renting an apartment, with a few additions. Folks who haven't rented in a while might not recall that there are regulations around rentals. Some provinces have a maximum allowable rent increase per year, although even that adds up over time. For example, in 2020 the rate in Ontario was 2.2 percent (before it was frozen for 2021 for pandemic relief). So, on the average price of $2,125 for a one-bedroom apartment in Toronto, that's an extra $46.75 per year, which doesn't sound that bad, but it does add up over five years to be an extra $233.75 and in 10 years to $467.50 annually (more actually, because the percentage increases compound). Another province that has a maximum allowable rent increase is BC, where the average one-bedroom apartment rental in Vancouver was $1,941 in 2020. In several other provinces, rent increases aren't even regulated.

There's also the unpredictability of landlords, who may be able to evict you if your building becomes a condo, or for other reasons—in hot markets there's a new trend dubbed "renoviction," where they are allowed to ask you to leave to renovate for a family member moving in. Another downside of having a landlord in a condo or rental situation is that they may not be as attentive to repairs as you would like. Sometimes there can also be rules on how you can paint or decorate in a space that you don't own.

Seniors' Residences

Yet another housing option for older people is a seniors' residence. While Statistics Canada shows that the majority of Canadians over 65 live in their homes, around 7 percent live in special care facilities, either long-term or residential care. For some, this choice may be necessary if medical care is needed. But the costs can be steep. According to the Canada Mortgage and Housing Corporation's Senior Housing Survey for 2020, the average cost of renting a standard space in a seniors' residence ranged from $1,844 per month in Quebec to $3,865 per month in Ontario. *Comfort Life*, a guide to retirement living and care, further shows that the range of costs for independent living in a retirement home can be as high as $5,800 per month.

Assisted living, where you are provided with a variety of services including housekeeping, meals, medication administration, bathing and dressing (different service offerings vary), can range from a low of about $1,500 to a high of $6,000. In assisted living, residents are only provided with the services they require; they are not necessarily provided with all of the listed services. Depending on the facilities and the level of care, assisted living can be expensive.

Keep in mind that there are lifestyle considerations relevant to this style of living. While there are people who may enjoy a communal atmosphere with planned social activities and a certain degree of care when you need it, often you do give up space or privacy in exchange for these things. For example, giving up the space of an entire home or condo in exchange for the room and balcony that constitutes individual living space in many retirement homes. But again, it's about options. For those who feel like they need support, remember that today's aging in place is easier and there are more services available, such as accessibility aids, ride-sharing or taxis, meal delivery or meal-in-a-box products, and everything from pet groomers to hired helpers who can come to your home.

And families are also eager to support their loved ones who would prefer to age in place, so don't just assume that your kids are thinking you should downsize. We had a client referred to us by a bank because her sons applied for a home equity line of credit to help fund care for their mother in her home. The sons were determined to support their mom in her desire to stay at home, even though they were financially supporting their own children through university. And yet, she owned a home worth $3 million in North Toronto! The problem was, the family didn't even realize that the CHIP Reverse Mortgage was an option. Now the client is funding her own care, and the sons are still able to support her emotionally without the added financial stress.

Home Equity Line of Credit (HELOC)

Probably the second-most discussed alternative to reverse mortgages are revolving lines of credit, called home equity lines of credit (HELOCs) or home equity loans (they are fairly interchangeable terms, except the line of credit can be a variable amount and the loan is usually a fixed amount with an end date for repayment). Because lines of credit are already a familiar part of the average person's financial universe, they tend to understand them better, since they may have used them in the past. That's why HELOCs come to mind more quickly than reverse mortgages. But both options satisfy the same need: to use the equity in your home as a source for generating funds.

Don't be mistaken, lines of credit have their place: they're good for very short-term borrowing. But the reverse mortgage can provide the same cash flow that borrowers are looking for, often with more senior-friendly borrowing requirements. To begin with, there are different qualifying criteria for the reverse mortgage than there are for the HELOC. So, you can qualify for the reverse mortgage simply because you own a house, whereas with the HELOC you additionally need to show your ability to service debt, as in, have some regular income. With lines of credit, you are expected to make payments monthly. By contrast, with the reverse mortgage you don't need to make a payment until you move.

Another thing that most people don't realize regarding the reverse mortgage is that we guarantee you can stay in your house. On the other hand, HELOCs are a "demand loan," meaning that it can be called for repayment at any time for any reason. For instance, if your income situation changes—say your spouse passes away and you had been relying on their pension income to service the debt—then the loan can be called if interest payments cannot be made. We've also seen it happen that the entire line of credit needed to be paid back right away so the house had to be sold. Or the widow keeps the line of credit, but it is set to a lower limit, say from $20,000 to $10,000. All these things can happen quickly, too, sometimes with as little as 30 days' notice.

EXPERT SPOTLIGHT: MICHAEL BECKETTE

Michael Beckette is the founder and former CEO and president of Mortgage Alliance (www.mortgagealliance.com).

What is Mortgage Alliance and what is the company's mission?

Mortgage Alliance is one of the biggest brokerages in Canada. Mortgage Alliance works with more than one hundred lenders annually, including traditional banks, monoline lenders, private lenders and smaller lenders. The company's mission is to try to maintain really good relationships with the lenders that they work with. Mortgage Alliance's goal for the consumer is to try to find the best possible products for them at the time they need it and to help them through a complicated time, when they're either buying a property or they're using mortgage credit to maintain real estate or build a portfolio.

How has the business changed over the years and what do you think of the current real estate market?

Every year there's change. Regulatory changes are going on all the time. For example, the Canada Mortgage and Housing Corporation thinks that there's a high risk to the housing market. I don't necessarily agree. Housing has proved to be a really secure investment for individuals and as a real builder of wealth. We've actually seen, even during COVID-19 so far, very solid real estate market prices in major metropolitan areas. Toronto specifically is still holding and growing. People are saying that there's a lack of inventory, but I'm thinking that there's still really strong consumer confidence in the real estate market at this time.

Your mother-in-law took out a reverse mortgage. How did she make that decision?

Many older homeowners are equity-rich and cash-poor. My mother-in-law is an example of that. She is really independent; she wants to live her own life. When my father-in-law passed away, they were equity-rich with almost a million-dollar property. But she does not have as much revenue as she would like, and she has bills to take care of. Instead of going to us or to other family, she wants to do it herself. And the HomeEquity reverse mortgage provided the opportunity for her to do it herself and stay in her property. She's in the Stouffville area, living in a bungalow in a managed community on a golf course. They have maintenance fees to take care of the property and amenities like a pool, community centre. She loves being there.

With a reverse mortgage, a surviving spouse is able to stay in the house. We ask you to notify us, but nothing changes. Same thing goes if one spouse moves into long-term care. In fact, funding this possibility is another good reason to use a reverse mortgage. Both homeowners would still need to have their names on the house title, of course. (In cases where an adult child also lives in the house—say a 90-year-old mother who lives with her 65-year-old son—the adult child can still use the reverse mortgage after the mother passes away, provided that the adult child also meets the required age minimum of 55.)

When the last surviving customer passes away and the house does need to be sold to pay off the reverse mortgage, HomeEquity Bank is not going to be knocking on a client's door the day after a loved one passes. We give the family up to 12 months to sell the house. We know that settling estates takes time, with wills, powers of attorney, executors and probate. We're not there putting up "for sale" signs the week after. And we are here for support if you need it.

Yes, you can sometimes get a lower interest rate on a HELOC, but rates aren't everything. We also compound interest semi-annually, whereas lines of credit compound interest monthly. While the HELOC may work if your financial needs are very short-term and specific, a reverse mortgage is often a better choice for those who wish to have funds accessible more regularly and want to avoid the worry of the loan being called or the bank changing the terms.

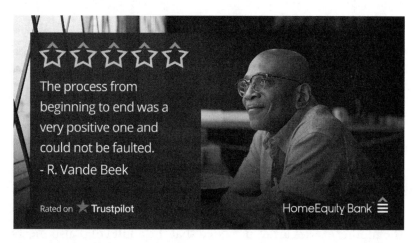

The process from beginning to end was a very positive one and could not be faulted.
- R. Vande Beek

Rated on ⭐ Trustpilot   HomeEquity Bank

Credit Cards and Other Alternatives

We just wanted to include a quick word about credit cards, even though people using them already know that they are not the best option. Even if you have a low-interest credit card, most of them still have higher interest rates than a line of credit, and some of them have astronomical interest rates like 20 percent or more. Same goes for second mortgages or other more-questionable loan options. People know they should avoid the downhill slope that these lead to, but we've met many now-customers who formerly relied on credit cards, and in some cases even on predatory lenders, because they thought they had no other options. They are so happy when they find out what is possible with a reverse mortgage!

Some will say that reverse mortgages have high interest rates and that there are better options. But the CHIP Reverse Mortgage stacks up for seniors. Yes, you can get a conventional mortgage or a line of credit (if you qualify) at a lower rate, but remember that you will have to make regular monthly mortgage payments. So, if you have cash flow issues, those are not real options. Other lending products start to get more expensive, not just with interest rates but also with fees. If you decide to pursue them, you should ask a lot of questions about fees and penalties. Some products out there have annual fees that can add thousands of dollars to your loan.

Credit cards or retail store cards should never be used to supplement cash flow. Not only are the interest rates high, but if you are good about making your minimum monthly payments on time, you can get rewarded with a credit limit increase. And so, for some it means the debt goes on and on and on.

Let's wrap up this discussion of alternative financial options with another story, one that incorporates an unfortunate number of the solutions outlined above. It's about a couple in their early sixties who lived in Kelowna, BC. One day, the husband had a massive heart attack and died instantly. The insurance paid off his debts, but he had always looked after the couple's financial affairs, and his widow knew nothing about financial matters and couldn't even balance a cheque book. She started receiving credit offers in the mail and responded to them.

The couple had a son who lived out of town. He visited his mother one day and found out that she had accumulated new debt in the amount of $40,000. She couldn't keep up with all the payments after the pension income was reduced, so the son took her to the local financial institution that his parents had dealt with for many years. They met with the branch manager and arranged a term mortgage to pay off the debts and gave the mother a credit card with a $5,000 limit.

Two years later when the son was visiting his mother one day, it was winter and he found that her gas had been turned off because she hadn't paid the bill. She was using a space heater to keep warm. The son couldn't understand why there was a problem. He did some investigating and discovered that the branch manager had given his mother a secured line of credit with a limit of $90,000 and a $15,000 credit card. The widow had maxed out the line of credit and the credit card.

Due to a poor housing market in the area and because she hadn't maintained the property very well, the widow's home could not be sold even after it was listed for six months. The son arranged for his mother to live with her daughter in Alberta. He cleaned out the home and took the keys and gave them to the branch manager, telling her that he didn't know what else to do. Could this widow have been better served with a reverse mortgage? Definitely. She might have been able to stay in her home for the rest of her life.

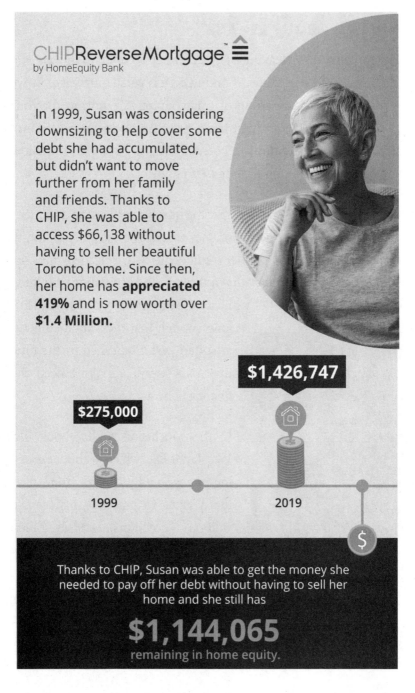

CHIPReverseMortgage™ ≜
by HomeEquity Bank

In 1999, Susan was considering downsizing to help cover some debt she had accumulated, but didn't want to move further from her family and friends. Thanks to CHIP, she was able to access $66,138 without having to sell her beautiful Toronto home. Since then, her home has **appreciated 419%** and is now worth over **$1.4 Million.**

$1,426,747

$275,000

1999

2019

Thanks to CHIP, Susan was able to get the money she needed to pay off her debt without having to sell her home and she still has

$1,144,065
remaining in home equity.

A WORD ABOUT LEGACY

The concern about leaving a legacy comes up often in the handful of reasons why people resist taking on a reverse mortgage. As we mentioned at the opening of this chapter, the notion that our clients are at risk of losing their houses is one of our most long-standing misconceptions to correct. We purposely do not allow you to borrow enough money to do that.

And yes, we're not surprised that the question of leaving an inheritance to children is one that comes up most often in speaking to financial planners. It's another tradition as rich as homeownership: the idea of passing money down through the generations, building on that family legacy. But while it's a lovely idea, today's seniors live long enough that their adult children are often well-established by the time they pass away, and don't need the financial boost.

Happy HomeEquity Bank clients the Hardeys.

In the conclusion to her book *The Well-Lived Life*, which is about exploring legacy in all its forms, from spiritual lessons to practical matters like wills and executors, Lyndsay Green writes about the fact that for so many of the people who she interviewed for the book, their departed family members and friends were still with them in emotional terms. She also urges readers to think of legacy as more than what they leave in their wills, noting "If we take our legacy seriously, we'll put our lives under a microscope and assess whether our pursuits and our behaviour are consistent with our goals and values. After this scrutiny, we might decide to refocus our lives to realize unfulfilled dreams where there is still time, or to follow new-found convictions." As a mother, I so prefer this idea of legacy and think it's one that could stand to get more publicity. Certainly, it's something on my mind when I pass along good financial habits to my daughters or every time we make memories together, from weeknight dinners at home to travel adventures.

Legacy is particularly interesting when it comes to reverse mortgages because, while we've met clients who are very concerned about passing something along to their children, for our average borrower in their seventies, typically their children are past the age where they need help buying their own house or establishing themselves in life. And we've seen many cases where the adult children themselves are the ones pleading for their parents to seek out a solution that will make their lives more comfortable.

Another thing: it's not like clients must make a choice between taking out a reverse mortgage *or* leaving money to their family. Our "No Negative Equity Guarantee" assures that. Also, if you review the examples of appreciation that we included earlier in the book, you'll see it's typically the case that house appreciation exceeds the interest owed. In over 99 percent of cases, there is money left over after the principal and interest get paid back.

You may be surprised to learn that many of our clients have taken out a reverse mortgage because they want to give money to their family immediately, so they can see them enjoy it before they die or make good use of it in some other way. For instance, when an adult child is going through a difficult time due to a divorce, an accident, an illness or some other hardship. In some instances, grandparents use the reverse mortgage to help pay for a grandchild's education. One favourite story around our company is about a grandfather from Ontario paying for a grandchild's medical degree in Australia.

Recently the term "Bank of Mom and Dad" has become very popular. The *2020 Home Buyers and Sellers Generational Trends Report* by the National Association of Realtors shows that 27 percent of homebuyers aged 22 to 29 and under (and 20 percent of homebuyers aged 30 to 39) sourced their down payment from a gift from a relative or friend. This percentage drops off in older age, although still 12 percent of the entirety of down payments are financed this way.

If you're thinking that skipping these worries about legacy means you can be selfish and selfless at the same time, you're right. Most people who you would pass your money on to don't *want* you to be thinking only about them. They want you to be a bit selfish in retirement, if only to make sure that you have all you need to be happy. And if we can cheerlead a bit here, too, it is *your* money—*you* made the smart decision to invest in a house early on and make it grow. *You* worked a lifetime on your career to earn that money. And *you* deserve to enjoy that earning—at minimum, not to live a life that's lesser than it should be, just for some dream of helping other people! If your family loves you, they will want your happiness and comfort more than they want your money. By the way, feel free to pass this rant along to any loved one who would benefit from it.

MEET THE TEAM: BARBARA MOODY, MORTGAGE SPECIALIST

One of the secrets to HomeEquity Bank's success is our caring team! We've sprinkled a handful of Q&As with team members throughout the book to help share even more client stories and perspectives.

What's your background?

I was a manager at another bank for 35 years. The banking system was changing so rapidly, and I just couldn't hop on board with all the changes, because I just didn't think it was customer-centric. I thought it was time for retirement. But I also knew a couple of people who worked for HomeEquity Bank. I decided it wouldn't hurt to spend half the day listening to what they offer. And oh, my golly, did I fall hard. I fell in love with the bank, the people. What we do is just so empowering. We're helping folks my age—because I'm in my sixties, too—to live their retirement dreams.

Who stands out as a memorable client?

I was talking to a lady in Nova Scotia who lived in her family home. Her parents had passed away, and she needed funds desperately because she was running out of money in her retirement. She needed to see a doctor. She had no money. She was bound to her home. She needed to see a dentist and she didn't have money for dentures.

You listen to these stories and you just have to help. This is *not* okay that people are living in these homes that have such great value, but they're still struggling. When we were able to get the approval, it opened up life for her. She can now go to her doctor knowing that whatever she needs, whether it's medicine or health aids, she has the cash to pay for it. She got herself some dentures.

We work our whole lives, so why, at the end of our time or in retirement, do we have to struggle? You know, there's lots of folks that take out the CHIP Reverse Mortgage to age in place. They're wanting to get those step-in tubs and grab rails and chair lifts, those types of things, because they love their home.

Why do you think there is still resistance to the reverse mortgage product?

I was recently at an anniversary party with a group of people who were the couple's family and friends. It became quiet just as dinner was being served. And I love to talk, so I said, "What does everybody think about the CHIP Reverse Mortgage?" Well, did that not get everybody all worked up! Many people were very indignant, saying, "I would never buy something if I couldn't pay for it." They were just really ignorant about what the product is, how it works. I think there's still a lot of those folks out there.

People think if you don't have the means, you don't do whatever it is. Or another fear is not leaving money to an estate. There are folks who just won't hear of it, even if they have a need themselves for more money. For example, I know of a couple where their only son passed away and his wife is trying to convince his parents to get a reverse mortgage, because she watches them struggle every month to make conventional mortgage payments and meet their expenses. And they're sitting in this nice home that's worth a lot of money. But they won't get the reverse mortgage because they say, "We want to leave our house to you when we're gone." Neither she nor her children need the money, and *she's* the one trying to convince them to help themselves.

FINANCIAL SENSE AND SOCIAL SENSE

So, back to the reverse mortgage. We're not asking that clients think only of the reverse mortgage, we're just hoping that it comes more quickly to mind and that they consider it as equally as any of the other options addressed in this chapter. Reverse mortgages make a lot of financial sense for those who have debt to pay off, especially when that debt is causing stress. They also make financial sense if you have specific goals for the money, from home improvements to an expenses cushion to bucket-list travel. They're even helpful when life burdens you with a new goal that you didn't know you had, like replacing the roof or buying a new car.

For many older Canadians, the thought of having to start over in a new community can be very stressful. There's evidence, too, that loneliness is a real threat to health and well-being. A 2019 National Poll on Healthy Aging conducted by the University of Michigan and sponsored by the American Association of Retired Persons (AARP) surveyed two thousand Americans aged 50 to 80 and found that about one in three reported a lack of companionship some of the time, with 27 percent feeling isolated from others during the past year. One in four reported social contact once a week or less. With these scenarios already a reality for some, it makes little sense to change your environment later in life if you can avoid it. Dr. Sinha says that loneliness is as bad for your health as smoking!

We have met so many people who have benefited from our product and even more who struggle and think they have no options. Oh, the worry that comes from thinking you have no options! I've met people who track their spending in extreme detail because they're so close to the line. But you wouldn't know it by looking at them—they look like they're doing fine. They're well-dressed and chatting about their grandchildren. But then they reveal that they haven't been to a social gathering in a couple of years because they don't want to be the only one showing up without a bottle of wine. We can't help but think that a CHIP Reverse Mortgage might be the right solution for them.

Another woman confided how she made up excuses not to see her grandchildren at Christmas. The real reason? She couldn't afford the flight. But she's living in a million-dollar home! In this case we're glad to report a happy ending: she qualified for a CHIP Reverse Mortgage and last year she did fly down to see her family. We're so pleased that she finally saw a reverse mortgage as an option that would work for her. That's our goal for others who we see suffering in the same way. We want them to look at our offering and think, *Why not me?*

CLIENT SPOTLIGHT: MARY W.

We've sprinkled a handful of Q&As with inspirational clients through-out the book to provide a sampling of the real voices behind people who have chosen the reverse mortgage.

How did you realize that the reverse mortgage might work for you?

I was never in charge of our finances. We live on a farm. My husband and I have a lot of horses, which are very expensive. It was a tremendous awakening and a great shock when our representative at the bank happened to come across the fact that we were using our credit cards, and the balances were getting quite high. And of course, the bank, they kept increasing our credit limits, so the problem was not getting solved. I found out that my husband and I, we had a second line of credit. I was in pretty dire straits when my banker mentioned the CHIP Reverse Mortgage, because I'd heard some things that I wasn't too happy about. But with the $50,000 second line of credit, I worried that we were facing foreclosure. I don't know exactly how close, but we were very close.

Besides consolidating debt, what else do you plan to do with the money?

We're going to take some money to fix our road, since there's a lot of potholes from horse trailers and trucks. And one of our barns, we noticed last year that there was a bit of snow coming in on the beams, so we've got to check that out. And some of the skylights may need to be replaced. It's practical things that we would have had trouble looking after.

What was your experience with HomeEquity Bank?

Our Mortgage Specialist was very good. He has a very good manner with people. He doesn't push. He talks—which I think is so important—he talks in layman's language. And I didn't feel stupid. I had quite a few stupid questions, believe me. I'm sure I'm not the only one that he has gone the distance for. He just strikes me as that kind of person.

Can you describe your property?

I have a large property: 24 acres with two road accesses and huge fields. It's an old ranch-style house, all on one level, which is what I need, not a lot of stairs. And we have huge barns. My husband has two tractors and he's always fiddling around with them, which keeps him busy. The house has huge, dark black beams in the ceiling and the wood is a blond colour. It's got large rooms, but it's very cozy. I have a nice den with a fireplace. It's old-fashioned. I've got a huge dining room table and huge china cabinet. And this is why I really would like to stay here. We have so many beautiful trees and bushes and so many animals, butterflies and skunks and opossums, rabbits, blue jays, hawks. It is very relaxing.

What has it meant to you to get a reverse mortgage?

I'm very happy that we did it. It's a great relief. It actually saved our life.

CHAPTER SIX

TALKING ABOUT MONEY

When my eldest daughter was in high school, a friend of mine, who is a money coach, talked to me about the power of giving kids a meaningful monthly allowance. So, I gave Sophie $160 every month, but I also handed over some expenses to her. I asked her to manage her monthly transit pass and cell phone bill, and I explained that she needed to cover those before she

Yvonne Ziomecki and her daughters, Sophie and Helen, with their dog, Butchy.

could spend on anything else. It was a great lesson on picking the best cell phone plan, budgeting for fun stuff and even little things that become big things later in life, such as making your lunch so you're not spending the money to eat out every day.

For university, I told both girls that I would pay everything for their first year, but in second year and beyond I would only pay tuition fees, so they would need to save money for food, accommodation and any treats. Sophie found a job at Starbucks before school even started. She continued to work through school, getting amazing jobs, saving money and learning to invest. She learned how to budget, how to plan her meals and how and where to grocery shop. She had to make difficult decisions about her housing, picking an apartment based on safety and affordability and not on fancy countertops and building amenities. I already know that Helen will follow in her sister's footsteps. She is very good at managing her money, can differentiate between needs and wants, and knows that experiences give you a lot more joy than material possessions.

These are just a few of the steps I took to initiate conversations about money with my children. As a mom, I want to raise confident daughters who see me taking care of my financial affairs and who also know that they can call on me if they have money questions or goals. I started by being upfront myself: I talk to them about my job in banking all the time. When I updated my own power of attorney and my will last summer, I talked to them directly about these important documents. I told them what my wishes are, both in financial terms and in terms of health care. I told them where to find copies of my will and which legal office I used to create it. By the time I did this, my straight talk about money was nothing new. After all, I'd already been offering for years to double their birthday money or allowance if they put the money in their savings account instead of spending it right away.

Do you have these family conversations about money? I think they're so important, yet I hear from so many people that they feel awkward bringing up the subject. That's especially the case for adult children who were raised in a family that never talked much about finances. I do relate to that. My conversations with my own parents have been less forthcoming. But you know what? I persist. I've asked whether they have a will, and even though they're a bit secretive on the details, they know from my openness that I'm willing to talk. And I'm reassured that at least the basics are in place. Financial sharing really depends on the individual, and I think that if we care about people, we at least need to make the effort to ask.

Being in this industry, and especially as a woman, I see all this stigma around women and money, so I want my daughters to be empowered with financial knowledge. I encourage questions and hope that even through my stories about work there is some learning by osmosis. Since my role brings me into contact with so many older people, I've met women who grew up at a time when there was even greater stigma around money, when caring and talking about finances may have been considered taboo and "unfeminine." I want my daughters to know that there's no reason to be shy when talking about money.

Even in the few years of age difference between my two daughters, I've seen more opportunities become available. I recently signed my younger daughter, Helen, up for financial literacy courses, something that's only now growing in popularity (just recently announced as an addition to the Ontario school curriculum, for example). She even got to try out an investor boot camp where she learned about the stock market! Having set the tone for these discussions, I'm pleased to report that my girls are now coming to me for advice on money—Helen has just asked about how to buy a car. She's growing up so fast!

Sophie's saving for a condo, something I strongly support. I'm pleased both because a condo will give Sophie something of her own and also because the real estate market is still such a solid long-term investment. When the time comes, I'm going to have lots of advice on how to choose the right place (smallest house on the nicest street is still my rule for new buyers). The cycle of homeownership continues!

YOUR FAMILY'S FINANCIAL CONVERSATIONS

Regardless of how you raised your children or how you were raised, today's families must find ways to talk more openly about money. At HomeEquity Bank, we really urge our customers to be transparent with their families when they are thinking about a product like a reverse mortgage. Obviously, our clients are adults, so we can't make them tell anyone their business, but it helps to have no surprises down the road. We even insist on independent legal counsel so there is at least one independent party as part of the transaction.

Since this is a topic that lots of clients have asked about and shared their own stories around, we have some helpful thoughts to share on how to do a financial conversation right, even when you're not in the habit. We've also shared some tips through the HomeEquity Bank website on this topic.

Some Thoughts on Talking to Your Adult Children

While many books seem to focus on how adult children can talk about finances with their elderly parents, we think a lot of the same rules apply to parents who want to talk to their adult children. As much as possible, try to have these conversations face to face. Choose a neutral time for the conversation. Many people assume that the holidays, when everyone is together, is the right time. We disagree. It's too busy and this conversation is too big—either the conversation will be swallowed up by the holiday or your children will be resentful thinking that you tried to take away from the celebration.

If possible, select a more neutral time when nothing is going on, and definitely choose a time when you're on good terms with each other. Maybe a weekend afternoon when you're both free. Also, don't think you can cover it in a 30-minute drop-in. You should probably even avoid asking your adult children to do any kind of chores at your place if that's your habit (we all love it when our tallest child offers to replace the lightbulbs!). The goal is to make the conversation completely neutral. Ask them to stay for the entire afternoon, and don't hit them with the topic as soon as they open your front door.

So, invite your kids over for tea or a meal. Or you can invite them to join you in an activity you both enjoy, such as gardening. Think about what you're going to say beforehand, but you don't need to be more formal than just laying out your financial plan and asking what they think. If you're talking about your house, maybe remind them of why you like the house and what fond memories you made there as a family. You might even bring out the photo albums and look at old photos of occasions at the house, reminding them of all the good times they had there as well.

Ideally, you should have this conversation after you've researched the reverse mortgage option and maybe even after you've applied, but before you've signed on, so that you can genuinely solicit their input. If you're having the conversation at a point when you've already made a decision and you're not so much soliciting information as you are keeping your children informed, you could say something like "I just wanted to let you know I'm applying for a reverse mortgage, so you feel like you're in the loop when I take action. I hope you will be supportive." Don't ask for a reaction right away, and don't rush the conversation.

If you have more than one child and different relationships with each, you might think about whether you want to discuss with one child first and the other(s) later. For example, a friend of mine was redoing her will in her sixties and she had two children, but one was really interested in financial matters and the other wasn't. She made the son the executor of her estate, and the daughter was actually fine with that! She was still transparent with both, of course, but didn't need to involve the daughter in all the details.

REVERSE MORTGAGES IN PARTICULAR

For the reverse mortgage conversation, think about the reasons why you're thinking about it or have decided to move forward with it. Outline the reasons why you feel that staying in your house is the best option for you, and tell your children about your plans for the money. If you haven't addressed this before, it might make you feel a bit awkward to be this transparent about financial matters, but we think the upside is that your children will feel happy that you've let them into your life a little more. They may even feel more comfortable sharing their own situations with you.

You should also be prepared to share your thinking on other options (such as the ones outlined in the previous chapter) and maybe the reasons you've decided to age in place. Your children may invite you to come live with them or suggest the D-word (downsizing!). Be honest with them about why you think the reverse mortgage may be a better fit for you. It's possible that your kids don't know much about reverse mortgages because they're not yet in that age bracket, so you could also have one of our brochures on hand to show them. Or, better yet, lend them this book!

Remember, if you haven't had these conversations before, it may take your children some time to think about what you're revealing to them, so be careful about demanding an instant reaction. Let them think about it. And know that you've made the first step towards greater transparency with them.

How Adult Children Can Talk to Parents

We've been addressing how parents can have conversations with their adult children, but we actually find that it's often adult children who contact HomeEquity Bank looking for better options for their parents. A great resource that provides tips on having these difficult conversations is personal finance journalist Cameron Huddleston's book *Mom and Dad We Need to Talk: How to Have Essential Conversations with Your Parents about Their Finances.* In it, Huddleston provides sound advice on how to frame conversations properly, including not making them about you, not issuing ultimatums and not being condescending. She also offers some good conversation starters. To indicate the size of the challenge, Huddleston quotes a 2016 Care.com survey that revealed more than half of parents would rather have the sex talk with their kids than talk to their parents about money and aging!

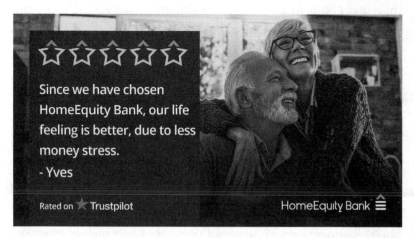

Since we have chosen HomeEquity Bank, our life feeling is better, due to less money stress.

- Yves

Rated on ★ Trustpilot   HomeEquity Bank ≡

Another somewhat more general resource is *Our Turn to Parent: Shared Experiences and Practical Advice on Caring for Aging Parents in Canada* by Barbara Dunn and Linda Scott, two women who took on roles as caregivers for their elderly parents. This book offers advice on how to determine if your parent needs more care, how to talk to parents and siblings about this topic, and practical tips both on how to help a parent age in place and move into care. The book also includes some helpful checklists, including how to assess and fix potential safety hazards around an aging parent's home, and a list of questions to ask when hiring a home-care professional.

QUESTIONS ADULT CHILDREN COULD ASK THEIR PARENTS

LEGAL: Who is the family lawyer? Do they have a will? Who will act as power of attorney?

HEALTH: Who is their health insurance provider? What is their family doctor's name? What's the state of their medical bills?

INCOME AND EXPENSES: What monthly income do they have? Do they have a financial advisor or someone that manages their money? Are there major expenses that need to be made each month?

DEBTS AND ASSETS: Do they own property that you don't know about? Do they owe a significant amount of money? How many credit cards do they have?

RECORDS: Where are the important records kept? Do they have a safe deposit box? Are there keys or passwords you should know?

For more tips on talking to aging parents about finances, see www.homeequitybank.ca/media/press-releases/talking-to-aging-parents-about-finance/.

We think that all the tips we outlined in the previous section apply equally for adult children trying to have financial conversations with their parents. If you have siblings, you should align with them in advance and decide on a proposed plan of action—you might want to select one of you to initiate the conversation, so it doesn't feel like an attack. Again, find that neutral time. Ideally you will have started the conversation early in your adult relationship with your parents, but even if you haven't, allow plenty of time on the day when you decide to broach this conversation. Consider discussing things over a meal (maybe you can bring the snacks to Mom and Dad's table) or some activity that you both enjoy, perhaps like gardening or puzzling.

Preface the conversation with a statement of support and affection. You might even use examples from within your family or community to convey that older adults are not alone in facing financial challenges. Come to the conversation already having done some background research; for example, on community resources that could be helpful. If there is a specific issue, maybe start by acknowledging it and the pain it is causing. If you're going to raise the reverse mortgage as a topic of conversation, consider bringing some of our brochures (or this book!) along with you. As with conversations initiated by the parent, you shouldn't expect that one chat will accomplish everything, and you should follow up the next day with a call or an email repeating key points.

An approach we sometimes like to take is linking these conversations to current events. For example, when a fraud scam targeting older people appears in the news, ask your parents if they've heard of it. That can be a good segue into talking about money more generally. Or when the COVID-19 pandemic hit and we saw all the awful news about long-term care homes, a lot of people were starting to have conversations about retirement homes and planning.

Again, you don't need to fix everything in their world. Starting a gentle conversation is often all that is needed. Using the news makes it even less personal, so you can talk in general terms and find out their opinion without making them feel like you are trying to investigate their personal affairs. If you hear them getting defensive, drop it and make a plan to follow up later. It's all about planting a seed.

Another way that adult children can help their aging parents is by being observant. Especially if a parent is living alone, there may be signs that they are having trouble with the upkeep of their home and may need help. Just keep an eye out for any changes that you might notice at your parents' home. We're not suggesting you should turn into a spy. Just start being someone who notices things. For example, if you notice items falling into disrepair, say the eavestroughs are falling off or the back deck really needs painting or there's a tile that's broken in the kitchen that they're not getting fixed. Notice whether there is more clutter than usual in their home. Burned pots or spoiled food can be another sign of change. You can also look out for personal elements. For instance, if they've lost weight or have become sloppy about their appearance, when once they were tidier. Not opening bills or paying them can be a sign of avoiding thinking about finances.

Now, you know your parents—if they've never been the type to fix the broken tile, or their personal style has always been jeans and a T-shirt, then it may just be in keeping with that pattern. Although you still might want to offer to fix that tile anyway or hire someone. (It's too late to change the T-shirts.) But if they were fussy before and now things are falling apart, it could be a financial and safety concern. Again, while you do need to have a conversation if you see these signs, you should still make every effort to set the right tone and not come across as judgmental.

People often worry that things falling into disrepair can be a sign of forgetfulness or an age-onset disease like Alzheimer's, which is also a concern. Either way, if you're noticing things, start to have those conversations, gently, and remember that finances can also be a factor. You might say something like, "Mom, I see the patio's in need of repair. Have you thought about getting the stones fixed?" If she seems open, you can probe a little further, "I think it will probably cost a few thousand. Do you have that money?" That sounds direct, and you might have to think of a softer approach. But it's worth trying to ask. Put yourself in their position, and you'll realize that it may be hard for parents to ask their kids for help, but when you've offered or at least raised the topic, it makes it's easier.

MEET THE TEAM: KRISTA ZINGEL, BUSINESS DEVELOPMENT MANAGER, CENTRAL TORONTO

One of the secrets to HomeEquity Bank's success is our caring team! We've sprinkled a handful of Q&As with team members throughout the book to help share even more client stories and perspectives.

What's your background?

I've been in the industry for 33 years. I started off as a banker and then a manager in Toronto, then I worked north of Toronto as a mortgage broker. When I returned to the city, I worked for the regulator. I've always been very much a social justice warrior and a strong consumer advocate. When I was working at another bank, I noticed this trend of clients being referred to me who were retiring with a lot of debt. We were positioning the home equity line of credit as a way to bridge that gap. I didn't feel 100 percent about it. I thought, this is a temporary solution. What about 10 years from now, or even five years from now?

So, I started researching the demographic, and it just got me thinking deeper. Looking at the stats, I thought, reverse mortgages are going to be the next big thing. If you told me before that I would be the new CHIP lady, I would have looked at you funny. But I convinced myself that this was going to be a really important product for Canadians and retirement. So, I called up the VP and had a meeting, and a month later, I was on the team.

What are some factors that stand out to you about your clients as a whole?

The boomer generation has faced economic challenges that previous generations were not faced with. The life expectancy is on an upward trend, the cost of living has gone up, while the value of our income has stayed the same. And pension benefits are drastically reduced. And then boomers have got their adult children who are facing economic challenges, student loan debt, or the fact that they can only afford about a third of the house that their parents can afford.

So, I think that this generation is being leaned on very heavily financially, and instead of putting on the oxygen mask—like how in a plane you're supposed to put on your own oxygen mask before helping someone else—and focusing on their own savings, every parent wants to help their children. So, there have been a lot of things that have been happening. And costs are up with the health care system. It's just a perfect storm.

But the good news is that the house you bought for $180,000 is now worth $800,000 or $900,000. We have to show them that this is actually where your savings are—it's not sitting in an RRSP or a RRIF, it's sitting in your house. And it's actually to your advantage to take tax-free money. As opposed to, if you do have investments, every time you take money out of a RRIF, it's subject to tax.

What do you like about working for HomeEquity Bank?

You very quickly learn, when you become a part of this company, about both the conscious and unconscious bias towards the product, not just with the general public and the end customer, but also our broker partners who specialize in home financing. People need permission to deal with their financial problems. People need to understand that they are in the same boat with a major percentage of retirees in Canada. They're in very good company, having debt. And there's a lot of shame surrounding debt when we're all told the big financial goal is to pay off your mortgage.

I like working at HomeEquity Bank because I'm making a lifetime impact. I'm taking people out of a situation that was beyond their control and giving them permission to live the rest of their lives with independence and dignity, and on their own terms. I can't think of a better place for me to be. It's what my core values speak to: consumer advocacy, product suitability and protecting a really vulnerable sector. I'm opening up people's eyes to alternatives to long-term care facilities. There are broader social issues that this reaches, and to be a part of the solution—I just can't think of a better place to be.

TALKING TO PEOPLE OUTSIDE YOUR FAMILY: IMPORTANT PROFESSIONALS TO CONSULT

Besides talking to your family about your reverse mortgage, it's also a good idea to talk to relevant professionals. At HomeEquity Bank, we insist that all our clients find independent legal advisors to review the transaction, and we're also happy to talk to any financial advisors that you may already have on your team. In fact, we called on some experts and expert sources for advice to include in this section.

Financial Advice

While our Mortgage Specialists are happy to speak with your financial advisor if you have one, we don't require that you hire an advisor in order to sign on to a reverse mortgage. Financial planners are one of those professionals that most people assume others have on call, but not all of us do. Many people figure they don't have enough money saved to warrant a financial advisor, or they just rely on someone from their bank.

Many of the financial planning questions that come up when considering a reverse mortgage are the same ones that arise when you start thinking about financial planning for retirement. There are a number of good books out there about retirement planning in general, from Suze Orman's recent *The Ultimate Retirement Guide for 50+: Winning Strategies to Make Your Money Last a Lifetime* (2020) to *Retirement Income for Life: Getting More Without Saving More* (2018) by Fred Vettese.

There are also many websites out there on financial matters, including official ones like the Financial Consumer Agency of Canada and Ontario's Get Smarter About Money. Be careful when looking online for financial information generally, though, because rules and products can be slightly different in different countries. Watch out also to note the date of any articles, as information can also change quickly.

Canadian money magazines such as *MoneySense* have useful articles and there are some decent financial columnists such as the *Globe and Mail's* personal finance columnist, Rob Carrick, and Jonathan Chevreau, who was a personal finance columnist for the *Financial Post* for nearly two decades and now runs the Financial Independence Hub. Personal finance blogs have become popular in the last few years. For example, *Boomer & Echo* and RetireHappy.ca.

One outstanding personal finance columnist is Pattie Lovett-Reid, chief financial commentator for CTV, who also writes a column for BNN Bloomberg. In her past columns about retirement, she looks at the five Rs of retirement planning, including *reassessing* your retirement and changing it if you're not in love with your situation; taking up the *rewards* of your retirement by spending and enjoying the money you have; finding a structure and social schedule that works for you in terms of how you spend your days; and *repositioning* your portfolio so you don't outlive your income. She also reminds us that in retirement, it's all about preservation of wealth rather than massive accumulation.

Lovett-Reid also has some tips for what *not* to do in retirement. She advises against retiring with debt or carrying a credit card balance. She also suggests that your senior years are not the time to start playing aggressively with the stock market. She does advise setting a budget in retirement, deciding when you're going to take your government pensions, and looking into any tax credits you might be eligible for. And any seniors' discounts too!

Retirement books and articles focus on factors like making a retirement-oriented budget and figuring out all your various sources of retirement income along with your anticipated expenses in retirement. Having those budgets in hand when you are planning your reverse mortgage application helps you to figure out how much money you might want to take out or what version might work better for you (for example, how our **Income Advantage** product for monthly withdrawals might work better for you than the traditional lump-sum reverse mortgage). The financial planner is the human upgrade from books, of course, because they can help you evaluate your specific situation and provide advice based on your particulars and their deep understanding of this world.

Chapter Five of Suze Orman's *The Ultimate Retirement Guide for 50+* is called "Power Moves for Your 60s" and has some good advice on considerations for planning your finances in this decade. Orman is American, so the advice relates to US financial products, but the actions and reminders map more generally to Canadian tools. She also devotes a full chapter to finding the right financial advisor, with questions and checklists.

If you do want to find a financial advisor of your own, we suggest finding someone who is well-versed in retirement planning as well as in other elder specialties, such as wills and estates. Ask about their credentials, how long they've been in business and whether they've served other clients like you. Ask about their fees. You might even ask if a financial planner has dealt with reverse mortgages in particular.

When you meet with your planner, bring a list of questions that you wish to clarify about your financial situation. For the reverse mortgage product, ask them to help you understand how it will fit into the rest of your financial plan, and ask any questions you might have about the contract or the product. You should feel free to share your financial documents and to ask them about other options they can recommend, and about other clients' experiences with the reverse mortgage.

Legal Advice

At HomeEquity Bank, we actually require an independent lawyer to review a client's CHIP Reverse Mortgage contract before moving ahead, just to make sure the client understands everything that's involved. We also want to have an independent party to verify that there's no undue pressure on the client. For instance, to make sure that their adult children or other outsiders are not pressuring them into taking out the money, or that they're not being coerced in other ways. We are wary of the variety of romance scams perpetrated on older adults these days.

When clients meet with the lawyer, it's one-on-one, so even if a potential client appears with their adult children, the lawyer asks to deal with the client directly to monitor for undue pressure.

We have definitely had cases in the past where an independent lawyer told us that we shouldn't go through with the arrangement for these reasons and more.

We ask you to bring your independent legal advisor (ILA) on once you've submitted your commitment package (including disclosure and application acknowledgement forms) to your Mortgage Specialist. HomeEquity Bank then sends your legal documents to your lawyer, and you schedule an appointment with your lawyer to review the legal mortgage documentation. That's your opportunity to ask any outstanding questions before you then sign. There is a list of documents you need to bring, including identification, a recent tax bill and others. (For the full list, see our checklist on the HomeEquity Bank website.)

You will leave the meeting with your ILA certificate and a copy of the legal documents signed by you and witnessed by your legal advisor. Once the legal documents have been signed and returned to HomeEquity Bank, your Mortgage Specialist will contact you with the availability of your reverse mortgage funds.

So that the legal advice is truly independent, the client is responsible for the cost of the ILA, which can be anywhere from $300 to $700. You may have a lawyer on call who you have used for other reasons, from house purchases to creating a will, but be aware that not all lawyers are well-versed on the reverse mortgage product (for instance, a tax lawyer might not know a lot about contracts). So, we encourage you to make an effort to find a lawyer who has experience in this area. Real estate lawyers or family lawyers are often the best. Usually clients are able to ask around and find a suitable lawyer in their network, but we also have a list of independent lawyers you can contact.

An independent lawyer will do a good job of explaining options to you, translating any elements of the contract that you don't understand and making sure you've asked us all the questions you need to ask in order to feel really confident in the transaction. Of course, HomeEquity Bank also has lawyers on our end, to verify information in the contract. We do a title search on your house to see if there are any liens and to verify your property tax, among other checks.

To help provide even more guidance in this chapter, we called on a lawyer who regularly advocates for and helps clients in all facets of family, estate and trust law, Mr. William Parker. He has also worked with several HomeEquity Bank CHIP Reverse Mortgage clients as their independent legal advisor. We asked Mr. Parker to comment on the kinds of questions that people can ask in order to find a suitable lawyer, the types of things he covers in a reverse mortgage conversation and the types of questions he has received about reverse mortgages. You can read his responses in the Expert Spotlight Lawyer Q&A sidebar.

EXPERT SPOTLIGHT: LAWYER Q&A
WILLIAM PARKER, B.A., B.P.H.E., LL.B., TEP

William Parker has been a lawyer in Toronto for more than 25 years and is the principal partner at Parker & Company (www.parkercompany.ca), which practices exclusively in the areas of family law, estate law and elder law. We asked him for advice on how to choose a lawyer for your reverse mortgage, and what questions you should ask.

What kinds of questions should a client ask before hiring an independent legal advisor?

I think a person should be looking to confirm that their prospective lawyer has a reasonable understanding of the area in which they will provide counsel. So, to hire a lawyer to look at a reverse mortgage, I'd look for someone who, at minimum, has experience with real estate, an understanding of mortgages and, ideally, a familiarity with issues relevant to the 55-plus demographic. In my case, looking at reverse mortgages falls under our elder law practice, which also includes everything from wills to power of attorneys to estate planning.

Are there elements that a lawyer should be familiar with when looking at a reverse mortgage document?

It's important that they know about the typical terminology around reverse mortgages. I'd ask how many reverse mortgages clients they have had and also whether they have ever been in a situation where they have recommended against someone taking on a reverse mortgage, or if they would be willing to do so.

Once a client has hired you, what do you look for in a reverse mortgage document and what points do you help clients understand?

I usually look over the document and explain to clients in relatively simplistic terms what the document outlines. I ask them about the amount of money that they want to borrow, what they want the money for, and a bit about their financial and personal circumstances: their age, their health, their marital status, whether they have any dependents, their assets and their debts, that kind of thing. I ask those questions not to be the financial planner or to "get into their business," but rather to understand why they're contemplating the loan, whether it makes sense for them and, importantly, to understand whether any red flags exist (for example, a lack of the requisite capacity to enter into the transaction, whether they are acting voluntarily, etc.).

Then I look at what the contract says about when they would have to pay the loan back and I make sure they know how much it costs them; in other words, an approximation of the total money they would have to pay back at certain periods of time. And then I make sure they are aware of any costs associated, from appraisal fees to my fee.

What are some questions that clients typically ask you?

Besides the basic questions like how much the loan will cost and what their obligations are, some questions I've had in the past include: When do they have to pay the money back? Do they have to live in their home? Can they rent their home out? Can they add their son or daughter to the title of their home for estate planning reasons? What happens if they get married later? What kinds of things must they keep the bank informed about? What happens if they're hospitalized and out of their home for a while? Can they make payments and, if so, what amounts? What happens if they want to move? What happens when they die?

Are there any questions clients shouldn't ask?

Not at all—I tell the clients that my job is to do a service and I will charge them for it, and that their job, being the customer, is to ask any questions whatsoever to help them ensure they are making the best possible decision for them in their circumstances. Having said that, however, some clients ask me to confirm a decision to borrow while maintaining other valuable assets, such as a second home. For example, one of my most memorable clients asked me if I thought the loan made sense, and when I suggested that he could sell his cottage instead, he replied "Oh, I can't do that—that's my Shangri-La." With my client's reply, I laughed and told him that he couldn't really then ask me if the loan made sense, because I couldn't value or even appreciate the enjoyment he gets from his paradise.

CHAPTER SEVEN

LIVING IN THE HOME YOU LOVE

Staying in your home as you age doesn't need to be taxing. There are hundreds of new appliances, gadgets and activities to make your life at home safer and more comfortable. And sometimes the smallest thing can make a huge difference, as the story I'm about to share demonstrates.

A few months ago, I was visiting an elderly relative who I see a couple times a year for major holidays and life events. While I was using her main-floor powder room, I noticed that once again, the toilet paper holder was hanging out of the wall. This was somewhat puzzling, but not for too long: turns out that the homeowner, a woman in her eighties, was using the toilet paper holder as a grab bar. Tiny screws and drywall were no match for her 130-pound frame. Thankfully, I had just finished a cross-country TV tour speaking about various gadgets and appliances that older people can use to make aging in place more comfortable and enjoyable. So, I had a word with her son, confidentially, and recommended that he look into Moen's line of home-care products—they offer a broad selection of tools and accessories that are functional and stylish, but most importantly, safe. Shortly after, a brand-new holder was installed and safely secured to the wall.

Another reason for seeking out safety and accessibility products that simplify and improve aging in place is the ongoing crisis in long-term care homes. In August 2020, the Canadian Institute for Health Information reported that one in nine long-term care residents potentially could have been cared for at home, noting difficulty navigating the health care system and financial barriers as some of the reasons for moving into care. And to quote Dr. Sinha from back in Chapter Four, "That little service that we could have started you on proactively could have prevented that big fall." To me, these little services are lifesavers and can make the difference between safety in your home and taking risks by working around repairs that you know you need to make. It's one of the best arguments for the reverse mortgage—to find that money you never thought you had to make your environment even safer and your life easier.

So, let's get started. From kitchen to bathroom to gardening to gadgets and services, we're going to feature many interesting products and tips that we've come across to help make the lives of older people easier. For any adult children reading this chapter, it is filled with good suggestions for future holiday and birthday gifts! Also, researching this made us realize that there are a lot more options than there once were. We've moved far beyond "The Clapper" (remember those TV commercials from the '80s?) to appliances you can control via your smartphone, and it is fantastic what is possible now.

We're also including more serious tips on how you can start a safety audit of your home. A 2019 report from the Canadian Institute for Health Information revealed that more than 137,500 seniors (age 65 and older) were hospitalized for injuries in 2017–18, with most injuries caused by falls. Falls accounted for 60 percent of all reported emergency room visits among seniors, with an estimated 20 percent admitted to the hospital. Most of the falls that prompted the reported ER visits (28 percent) occurred at home.

We've rounded up safety tips aimed at danger zones like the kitchen and bathroom—many of which are useful for any home, for any generation! As we age, anything we can do to help our future selves is useful. And again, to the adult children: What nicer gift could you give than to help your parents assess their home hazards? With their permission, of course.

Another reason we're writing about safety and ease of access is that some of these renovations can be very necessary for those who are serious about keeping their home into old age. In their book *How to Age in Place: Planning for a Happy, Independent, and Financially Secure Retirement,* Mary Languirand and Robert Bornstein include a chapter on making your home safe with important advice about universal home design, a term used to describe living spaces that help people with various challenges live independently. These authors also include tips on fixes that will help if you're prone to aging-related memory loss, and some clues to tell if your memory loss is more serious.

Renovations are a major way that our clients use their reverse mortgage money, from fixes that make their home safer, to dream kitchens and bathroom renos that help create the home they've always wanted (and boost their house value in the process!). In fact, a 2016 study conducted by Ipsos and HomeEquity Bank of three hundred Canadian homeowners showed that 58 percent felt they would need to renovate to remain in their home, and 11 percent noted it would require major renovations. Furthermore, 44 percent said renovations would be needed for their kitchens or bathrooms, to improve accessibility. To share some tips about what you should look for in a contractor and what may be possible for a home renovation, we reached out to accessibility contractor Pat Acquisto, who provides answers to some frequently asked questions in the sidebar "Spotlight on Accessibility," which appears later this this chapter.

But before looking at fixes by area, let's consider a couple more stories. A few years ago, we received a letter from a son of one of our clients. His mom took out a CHIP Reverse Mortgage for the sole purpose of renovating her very dated kitchen. He sent us a picture of the new-and-improved space: it was a first-class renovation and the results looked very inviting. But the best part? He said that his mother changed so much since the kitchen reno. He said that she never answers his calls anymore, which sounds like a bad thing until you learn that it's because she's busy cooking, baking and entertaining. Her kitchen is full of friends over for coffee, lunch, dinner, you name it. He was so grateful and even emotional to see his mother so happy again.

Yet another client who used renovations to age in place is a 91-year-old living in North Vancouver. Her house is worth $1.8 million. She used her CHIP Reverse Mortgage to completely renovate her home with handrails, assistive furniture and a ceiling track system to help her in and out of bed. She also created a monthly cash flow for meal preparation and house-cleaning services. Today, her three daughters are happy and stress-free because she's taking care of herself! Regardless of your budget, there are many things you can do to make things safer and more accessible in your home.

And while you're improving your life, yet another place to make things fun is travel! It's one of the most rewarding ways to spend money, so we've also included some thoughts on that topic near the end of the chapter. While many clients borrow money initially for more practical things, many also realize eventually that accessing the equity in their homes gives them a bit more room in the budget for some bucket-list travel! Why not add some adventure?

LET'S START IN THE KITCHEN

While we're highlighting in this section some gadgets that work for older people, we'll talk mostly in terms of categories and types of inventive products now on the market. We're not always going to name brands or specific names because those can come and go, but instead we want to help you learn what kinds of products are available. Your job is to seek them out in your own neighbourhood stores or online.

Midnight Scoop and Other Gadgets

Occasionally we will call out a product by name, if it's particularly unique or just fun. The first example in that realm is the Midnight Scoop. What's great about this product is

Midnight Scoop!

that it takes a gadget we're all familiar with, the ice cream scoop, and rethinks it in the interest of older people. In this case, the product entirely changes the way you scoop ice cream. Rather than the traditional method of pulling the scoop towards you, this new tool has the user push on the curved end of the handle, to use your stronger arm muscles. It's great for weak wrists! Designer Michael Chao (who called the product "Midnight Scoop" because of the fact that he stayed up late nights perfecting it), made the tool out of aerospace-grade aluminum with a lifetime warranty so that you can hand it down to other generations.

A similarly genius invention is the **one-handed bottle opener**, for those who have trouble with a bottle opener but can pull a trigger. This gadget lets you hook your second finger in a trigger-tip and then lift the cap up and away. And it's made of magnetized metal, so the cap doesn't roll away. There are also ergonomic and even automatic wine bottle openers.

Staying in the genre of opening containers, many of us have seen the classic automatic can openers, but did you know there are now **automatic jar openers**? To use one, you place the device atop a jar, and outer arms grip the jar while inner arms clamp around the lid and rotate it. The device works on a variety of jar sizes. There are also bag openers that allow you to more easily open things like chip bags or bags of frozen vegetables.

And there's more. Actually, the social platform Pinterest.ca is a great place for looking for accessibility ideas. So are online companies that cater to accessibility needs. Here are just a few more kitchen products that actually exist: a perching stool if you get tired of standing, measuring cups with large print, measuring spoons that are colour-coded differently for each size, extra-large digital-number cooking timers, plates with large lips and non-skid bottoms, cutlery with ergonomic grips, tactile microwave stickers, and knorks (that's knife plus fork). You can even get a kettle tipper for safely pouring hot water!

Some Other Great Kitchen Tips

Other tips for the kitchen are not ingenious inventions but, rather, common sense applied to this space in the interest of the older kitchen user. And we do want to keep these queens and kings of the kitchen comfortable because they make such great food in there! The following are a few ideas.

Add More Light

Since eyesight weakens with age, adding proper task lighting around your kitchen can avoid accidents. Many range hoods already have lights (so use them!) and lighting up your other regular use areas, such as sinks and countertops, can also help. Having light switches at each entrance to the kitchen ensures we are not feeling around in the dark. Did you know that you can even buy LED faucet lights that shine red when the water pouring from the faucet is hot and shine blue when it's cold? Great for avoiding scalds.

Pay Attention to the Stove

This is a tip for any age, but generally be aware of what is on and around your stovetop. Tie back billowy curtains and keep plastic away. Make sure that the controls on elements such as ovens are clearly marked (we all know these sometimes rub off with age). If need be, invest in a new stove that has accessible dials for people in wheelchairs.

Look for Places to Automate

Invest in automatic shut-off appliances to protect yourself even more from fire hazards. You may already have a kettle with automatic shut-off, but did you know there are a variety of devices available to install on your stove to automatically shut it off or to monitor when it hasn't been shut off? Using a variety of technologies from sensors to timers, some of these tools can go as far as automatically pouring fire suppressants onto the stove and turning it off. Others will send a notice to an app on your phone and the phone of your emergency contacts to alert them that the stove is still on.

Create Accessibility-Friendly Work Spaces

Everything from choosing countertops that are not too glossy (so they don't blind someone with declining vision), to installing faucets with levers that require less grip to operate, can help make the kitchen more user-friendly. Anti-fatigue floor mats can help to reduce pressure on feet, knees and lower backs, plus provide a grippy and stable surface for standing in meal prep areas. Cutting boards with suction grips underneath can help keep them attached to your counter.

For larger renovations, elements to consider include installing pullout drawers that let you see everything at a glance (and reduce reaching) and moving the sink closer to the stove so that you don't need to carry pots of hot waters a long distance. Choose a shallower sink for easier cleaning and rinsing, and keep the microwave at counter height to minimizing bending and reaching.

IN THE BATHROOM

The bathroom can be your personal spa, your reading room or the place where you wash your cares away in a hot bath after a long day. But as we age, it can also be a place of danger. Again, there are elements you can add to help to restore it to its original state of sanctuary. (Our Q&A with accessibility contractor Pat Acquisto in the sidebar provides even more tips.)

Grab Bars and Other Bathtub Helpers

Grab bars are often the first thing people think of when they consider bath safety, and for good reason. They help you to get in and out of the tub and to steady yourself when reaching for the shower knobs. Experts furthermore caution not just to use your towel rack—these are often not securely fastened, not designed to hold your full body weight and may come out of the wall, causing injury!

If you're not ready to commit to grab bars right away, today they make versions that lock on the side of your tub for extra stability or standing ones that go floor to ceiling if you need a grab bar but there's not a permanent place to install it. Yet another great accessory for grab bars is gripping tape, which helps to make grab bars even more grippy if your hands are wet or oily. Anti-slip bathtub coatings, stick-on grips or even bathtub mats can also help make the tub a safer place to stand. These are not just for children! They're practical for all tubs.

Portable Shower Heads, Shower Chairs and Toilet Safety Frames

For anyone who is less steady on their feet, why not find ways to make bath time easier? Portable showerheads make it easier to sit while bathing, and there are specially designed shower chairs that make bathing less of a chore for people with weaker legs. Installing a walk-in tub or shower can also be a good option for those who have difficulty stepping over the side of a traditional tub, and many come with seats built in.

A toilet safety frame provides helpful support when using ___ toilet, and they are available to suit different toilet heights and widths. For a low-cost improvement, you can buy toilet seats that fit your existing toilet and elevate the height by a few inches.

Other Great Tips to Make Your Bathroom Safer

Pay attention to water temperature by turning on the cold water first, before the hot water. Age plus some medications and health conditions can make your skin less sensitive to heat and at risk for burns. If you use a bathmat, make sure that it has a non-skid bottom so that you don't slip, and replace it when the rubberized backing wears out. You can also use a weighted shower curtain to prevent water from spilling out on the floor, something that creates another slipping hazard.

Reduce clutter generally in the bathroom. Keep toiletries within arm's reach so you avoid stretching (you could lose your balance) or bending down. Put a light-sensitive night-light in your bathroom so you're never in the dark (night-lights all over your home are a good idea). Bring your phone into the bathroom so you can get help quickly if you do fall while bathing.

For those who worry that grab bars and other safety gear aren't very . . . well, *sexy*, it turns out that companies are starting to pay attention to style in this area. Promenaid, founded by retired Montreal architect David Reich, offers handrails that are sleek as well as practical. Ottawa-based Invisia designs and manufactures bathroom accessories with accessibility built in. Brampton, Ontario–based Savaria sells a glass-walled elevator with a sleek look, called the Vuelift.

THINGS BOOMERS WILL REMEMBER

- Watching *I Love Lucy*
- Beatlemania
- Dialing a rotary phone
- Smoking on airplanes
- Looking something up in an encyclopedia
- Waiting for the milkman to deliver to your house
- Seeing TV channels sign off at the end of the night
- Shopping at the five-and-dimes
- Talking to an operator
- Seeing billboards advertising tobacco
- Eating weird Jell-O mould dishes
- Watching the first season of *Saturday Night Live*
- Looking up a number in a phone book
- Holding a sit-in to protest
- Listening to a transistor radio
- Using a typewriter
- Using a knob on the TV to change the channels
- Using a pay phone
- Buying your first vinyl record
- Looking through the Sears catalogue

Adapted from www.goodhousekeeping.com/life/entertainment/ g20074870/baby-boomer-facts/?slide=40

IN THE GARDEN

When we ask our clients how they like to spend their leisure time, gardening is a top answer. That's in spite of all the bending and walking that you need to do out there! Fortunately, there are many great gadgets today to help with the aspects that slow you down, starting with elevated garden beds that avoid the need for bending much at all. Here are some others:

Ergonomic Tools: Weeders, Soil Scoopers and Bulb Trowels

Designed for people with a weaker grip, ergonomic hand tools shift the workload onto your stronger arm muscles, and their thicker-diameter handles are easier to grip for someone with arthritis.

Gauntlet-style Garden Gloves

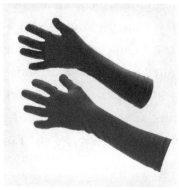

Lee Valley garden gloves

It seems that gauntlets are not just for knights anymore, but also for those who may have thinner skin on their arms and need protection for those protruding veins. Anatomical pads on the hands provide a more comfortable grip.

Garden Kneelers

From a padded foam-style that you put on the ground to a collapsible steel-frame-plus-fabric-stool style that you sit on, kneelers are designed to save tired knees and legs.

For the Indoor Gardener

Today's indoor herb gardener or seedling planter has many options, including small greenhouses that fit on your kitchen counter. Many are self-watering, and some come with pre-seeded plant pods that can be used for enjoying indoors or for raising seedlings to take outdoors.

IN-HOME TECHNOLOGY

"Hey, Google, what's the temperature outside?" Also, "Hey, Google, isn't it amazing that a machine can accurately answer questions like that?" Appointment reminders, calls, medication reminders—there are so many ways you can use smart technology these days, from Amazon Alexa to Google Home. Today, many smart thermostats can be operated from your smartphone and integrated with smart devices like Alexa. You can even auto-schedule your home temperature, automatically lowering it while you're away and see your energy-use history so you can keep an eye on your bill.

PC Magazine's Smart Home Device 2020 list includes a number of other technologies on the rise, from smart plugs that turn regular appliances into smart ones controllable from your phone, to smart door locks and doorbells you can control with your phone, too. Air conditioners, microwaves, sprinklers and vacuums are all appliances that you can now control with your phone or your voice.

Oh, and one more, for those of you who are constantly misplacing your keys or phone (isn't that everybody?), another fun gadget is Tile. It's a thingy you attach to your keyring or stick on your phone to help track it down via Bluetooth signal.

ADAPTABLE CLOTHING

Yes, companies are making clothing that's easier to use! And they're stylish. Tommy Hilfiger's Adaptive line features shirts with magnetic buttons for easy closure, jackets with one-handed zippers that are magnetized at the base, and pants and shorts with cord-lock fasteners on the drawstring designed to be operated with one hand. There are also Velcro-fly jeans. Plus, all of these items come with tons of internal pull-up loops to help you put these clothes on more easily.

Wide-fit and easy-open slippers, slip resistant socks, front-open bras, side-open pants . . . there are many other forms of accessible clothing these days to check out from a variety of retailers online.

CHIP Health

Let Your Home
Take Care of You

With a CHIP Reverse Mortgage, you can use your home's equity to afford a range of health and wellness expenses, including prescription drugs, alternative therapies, post-surgery recovery or ongoing care for a chronic illness. You'll also be able to pay for the upkeep and retrofits needed to stay in your home.

Health & Wellness

Prescription drugs	$450/year[8]
Private health insurance premiums	$550/year[8]
Gym membership	$800/year[9]
Massage, physiotherapy & acupuncture	$700/year[9]

At-Home Care[9]

Post-surgery care	$1,000 – $3,500/month
Personal care worker or nurse	$12,000 – $42,000/year
Overnight or live-in care	$58,000 – $75,000/year
24-hour in-home care	$200,000+/year

Home Maintenance[9]

Cleaner every 2 weeks	$3,120/year
Grass cutting or snow removal	$1,200/year
Monitoring system	$1,000/year
Pool opening, closing & monthly cleaning	$2,000/year

Home Improvements & Mobility Aids[9]

Stair lift	$1,200
Ramps	$8,000
Cane or walker	$150 – $400
Scooter	$2,400
Wheelchair	$4,000
Curbless shower or walk-in tub	$5,000
Kitchen reno	$25,000

8. https://cupe.ca/pharmacare-public-solution-rising-drug-costs; 9. www.chip.ca/reverse-mortgage-resources

Health & Wellness	
Prescription drugs	$450/year[8]
Private health insurance premiums	$550/year[8]
Gym membership	$800/year[9]
Massage, physiotherapy & acupuncture	$700/year[9]

At-Home Care[9]	
Post-surgery care	$1,000 – $3,500/month
Personal care worker or nurse	$12,000 – $42,000/year
Overnight or live-in care	$58,000 – $75,000/year
24-hour in-home care	$200,000+/year

Home Maintenance[9]	
Cleaner every 2 weeks	$3,120/year
Grass cutting or snow removal	$1,200/year
Monitoring system	$1,000/year
Pool opening, closing & monthly cleaning	$2,000/year

Home Improvements & Mobility Aids[9]	
Stair lift	$1,200
Ramps	$8,000
Cane or walker	$150 – $400
Scooter	$2,400
Wheelchair	$4,000
Curbless shower or walk-in tub	$5,000
Kitchen reno	$25,000

8. https://cupe.ca/pharmacare-public-solution-rising-drug-costs, 9. www.chip.ca/reverse-mortgage-resources

SERVICES TO MAKE LIFE EASIER

Another thing that makes life easier in the home is outsourcing some of your chores. Now there are apps for chores like lawn care and snow removal alike. Snow removal seems almost essential to hire someone else to look after, given all the warnings out there that correlate snow shovelling with heart attacks.

173

Other tasks like ordering food for delivery with apps like Skip the Dishes or Uber Eats are just nice to have. (But they are *really* nice to have.) Meal kit services like HelloFresh or GoodFood offer the opportunity to try new recipes with all the food pre-chopped and measured. Grocery delivery services from your local store or online services like Grocery Gateway or Instacart (some of these are affiliated with familiar Canadian grocery chains) allow you to make a permanent digital shopping list and get groceries delivered on a regular basis. Uber and Lyft have lowered the price of transportation and raised the availability of drivers on call.

General service providers like Fivrr and TaskRabbit have made it possible to hire for anything from handyperson services, to assembling IKEA furniture, to moving heavy objects around your home, to waiting in line for you. For those who need more care help in the home, companies like Nurse Next Door or Senior Helpers can provide services from meal prep to companionship to dementia care. Community services tailored to older people such as Meals on Wheels are great to look into, too! The Government of Canada also maintains a good list of services and programs online at www.canada.ca/seniors.

A WORD OF CAUTION

Even though technology can be wonderful, we're also aware of its downsides. Be wary of any tools or apps that seem too good to be true. There are scammers out there who are trying to find ways to trick Canadians. If you hear of a service that sounds too utopian, ask around to see if your adult children (or maybe grandchildren, who are often more up-to-date on current technology) have heard of it before, and get some recommendations.

We feel so strongly about protecting our clients from fraud that HomeEquity Bank commissioned a survey from Ipsos on the topic, which revealed that 91 percent of Canadians 55 years of age or better believe they are now more vulnerable to scams. We also created a video series called "Catch the Scam," where security expert Frank Abagnale (the subject of the film *Catch Me If You Can*, starring Leonardo DiCaprio) walks viewers through the pitfalls of the CRA scam, the grandparent scam, lottery scams and romance scams. The Government of Canada's Anti-Fraud Centre also tracks ongoing scams and frauds.

BACK TO MAKING YOUR LIFE EASIER

People often think of taking out a CHIP Reverse Mortgage as being a big financial decision only suited for people in financial difficulty who need to pay off debt or who have a large, unexpected expense such as car or roof. But the truth is that our reverse mortgage products are very flexible and can be used to satisfy any need and pretty much any situation. With our **Income Advantage** product, you get approved for a fixed amount, but you have an option to draw a monthly (or quarterly) income as little as $1,000 per month. Interest only accumulates on the amount drawn.

Some of our clients use the reverse mortgage to improve their cash flow and to afford to stay in the home they love. They hire a cleaner, someone to look after the lawn in the summer and someone to clear the snow from the driveway in the winter. They get some meals prepared, hire a handyperson to fix up small things around the house. Some have a pool (mostly for the grandkids), and those cleaning services are not cheap. We've heard people say, "My home is my pension plan." And why not?

WHY NOT TRAVEL?

Among the fun things people have done with their reverse mortgages, travel is at the top. I always smile when clients feel the need to inform us that they are being modest with their travel, or only going places that fit within their budgets—I think any travel is amazing! It's your business if you want to start seeing the world.

Growing up in Poland, we didn't have much room to travel, only within the Eastern Bloc. Still, I remember from childhood going across the border to the Czech Republic (Czechoslovakia then) and summer vacations in my teen years to Croatia. My sister Gosia and I always had so much fun exploring new places. After I came to Canada, a lot of my travel was focused on going home to Poland to see my parents, but eventually I would build on extensions to visit Paris or Prague.

When I worked at American Express, I would travel all over the world for work—New York, London, Mexico City, Hong Kong, Japan, France. I've also travelled with my daughters, which built even more great memories for our family. A few years ago, we flew to Calgary, rented a car and drove to Banff, then Jasper, then through Kelowna to Vancouver. We kept a leisurely pace and at night we'd play games in our hotel room. It was one of those trips where you

enjoy the drive and the journey as much as the destination. My spouse and I have travelled to some interesting places such as Havana, Memphis and London, and we have a very extensive wanderlust list on standby for when the pandemic is under

Yvonne Ziomecki and her daughters, Sophie and Helen, on the road in Banff, Alberta.

control. I feel like I inherited the travel bug from my parents, and I hope it's contagious enough to pass along to my children.

Many of my clients are immigrants like me and long to revisit their former country, whether it be in England or Europe or Asia or elsewhere. And some older people have deferred the dream of travel: they've meant to go someplace for years, but they kept getting wrapped up in the daily life of raising children and working. Some of them even confide that they realize now that their time on earth is shrinking and it's high time to visit their birth country or some bucket-list destination. That's why I was so pleased when a client of mine, who I mentioned earlier in the book, went to Spain at 86. He said he'd been thinking about it for years!

Many older people like to go on bus tours where the planning is done for you, to pick a destination and an itinerary and let the tour company do the rest. When we talk to a client after they've started to take action on their travel plans, they are so relaxed and happy about it. Planning new trips gives people something to look forward to, and taking trips helps people make new friends. They come back with fascinating stories they can tell over and over. Travel totally keeps people active and young at heart. What's better than that?

SPOTLIGHT ON ACCESSIBILITY: PAT ACQUISTO

Pro Accessibility (proaccessibility. ca) is a construction and project management firm that specializes in designing and modifying homes for seniors and people with disabilities or physical limitations. The firm holds the Certified Aging-in-Place Specialist (CAPS) designation, among others. The company is headquartered in Vaughan, Ontario, but has offices in several major cities across Canada, including Winnipeg, Calgary and Vancouver.

Accessibility construction specialist Pat Acquisto.

What is the benefit of hiring a contractor who specializes in accessibility?

I always tell people, never compare us to "Joe with the pickup truck," because, yes, he may be good at what he does, but he doesn't specialize. And in the type of work that we do, we're focused on understanding any medical conditions, coming up with solutions and translating those into construction terms. A lot of contractors may not have that experience and understanding of what multiple sclerosis is or what muscular dystrophy is, and what questions to ask to come up with a smart solution.

How do I find the right contractor for me?

You definitely want to make sure to assert your due diligence—do background checks to see if they have any specific certifications with dealing with accessible modifications. And also see if they have a proven track record. There are a lot of groups, such as Facebook groups, on this topic of accessibility, so you want to do your homework to see who other people have worked for, and make sure that they specialize in this type of work.

What are some general questions you ask potential clients?

We want to understand their disability: whether it is something they will get over, how it affects their mobility. There's a whole slew of questions we ask before we actually come up with a solution for them. For an older person, the first questions we ask are how long they see themselves living in the home, and whether it's a temporary solution or more long-term. And we also need to know what type of budget we're working with. We ask questions over the phone, and then typically there's a site meeting.

Pro Accessibility renovation: bed chair to assist in lifting from bed.

We like to speak with not just the clients but also the whole family because people tend not to consider the actual people who are involved in their day-to-day routines. It's not just the person aging or the person with the disability that's been affected. It's the family, the son, the daughter, the relatives, people visiting. The solutions we come up with will definitely affect and make everyone's life easier.

What are your most common renovations, and who generally calls you to get started?

The most common renovations by far are those that help in getting in and out of houses. And bathroom renos. And I would say 90 percent of calls are from the caregiver. A lot of times, seniors don't want to admit that they're getting old and that they have a disability.

What is involved in getting in and out of the house—would that be ramps?

A lot of times ramps unfortunately don't work, because of the height difference of the house. There's a rule of thumb that for every one-inch rise you want at least 12-to-16-inches run. So, if your typical house is two feet high, you need a 20-foot minimum ramp. Typically, people don't have that amount of space at their front lot, nor do they want to see a 20-foot ramp. So, if that's the case, we might use what's called a vertical platform lift. We can install it outside on their front porch or in their garage.

What is involved in a typical bathroom modification?

Definitely we look at the entrance door, to see how easy it is to get in. And while your typical bathroom has the bathtub and toilet, usually we want to remove that bathtub and create what we call a seamless shower transition. So, there's no height differences, no curb, it's just a smooth transition into the shower.

Then the types of toilets can vary depending on the user's height and their limitations and the disability. We can go with a higher toilet. The bathroom sink usually has a vanity below and a sink on top. Often, we want to remove that vanity. With the bathroom faucet, it's always good to have a single lever versus a dual lever. Just makes it a bit easier to handle.

When it comes to colour, and also the texture of the tiles, I'll make sure that it's more of a matte finish to improve the traction. We want to use contrasting colours on the floor and walls, in case the client has a vision impairment. Then they can see exactly where the floor ends and the shower begins, and where the wall ends and the sink begins. Having those slight changes in colour makes a huge difference. And you want grab bars in your main areas, always with solid backing behind the tiles.

Are there any renovations that people don't think of?

A lot of the lifting devices like elevators, or something called a telecab, which is a lifting device from one level to the next. They've come a long way in terms of the technology and in terms of price point. Doing the math and breaking it up over time, this tends to be a lot cheaper than potentially relocating.

Are there financial assistance programs that can help with these renovations?

Yes. The most popular is from the March of Dimes. That program is set up for people who have a lower income or are retired and collecting a small pension. If they're approved, they'll get up to $15,000 in one-time support towards any accessible home modification. There are also offers for vehicle modification, which we also do. The federal government offers the home accessibility tax credit for renovations that reduce the risk of harm in the home. Some provinces have additional programs.

How long does a construction project take? And how much does it cost?

It depends on the scope of work and what exactly we're doing. Your typical bathroom, from start to finish, will probably take between two and three weeks. We've done new houses from dirt to roof and move-in-ready. For that, you're probably closer to five or six months.

Your typical bathroom is probably five feet by eight feet, so you're looking at starting at $15,000. Depending on selections and layout and overall dimensions.

How do clients react when they see their new modifications?

I'm inundated with messages or emails or pictures. These implementations dramatically changed their lives. I have one client where the husband is six-foot-three, diagnosed with MS. He's a senior. His wife is almost his same age. She's five-foot-two and frail. There's no way that she can lift up her husband from the bed chair onto the wheelchair. So, we installed what's called a ceiling lift, which is a track that gets mounted to the ceiling. So now, mechanically, she can go pick up her husband: the motor does all the work. Without that, it would be virtually impossible for her to move her husband. They definitely feel safer staying at home versus going into long-term care.

Pro Accessibility renovation: walk-in shower with grab bars.

What do these modifications do for the resale value of the home?

I think it's the best investment you can ever make, and I'm not just saying that for business. The inventory of ready-to-go, accessible homes is maybe 0.1 percent. But the demand for accessible homes for resale is huge! Your house may increase in value because of the modifications, but it's also going to be off the market that much quicker because the demand is so high. Today for some realtors, that's all they do, specialize in finding people accessible homes.

Do you think it's better to age in place or go into a long-term care facility?

I go through the math of what it costs to stay versus what it costs to relocate or be in an old-age home. A lot of times they are sacrificing location to get something that they kind of like, but they still have to dump in money. And long-term care is probably a minimum of $5,000 a month. I bet you if you give me whatever you pay into long-term care for a year, give me half of that and I'll help you stay at home for the next 10 years. Our business in the last five years has doubled or tripled.

CHAPTER EIGHT

RESPECT YOUR ELDERS

Like many people, when I was younger I was afraid of getting older, of the aches and pains and health problems, of looking old. Now as I enter my fifth decade, I try not to think about aging in terms of numbers. Instead, I ask

Yvonne Ziomecki
relaxing in her backyard.

myself: *Where am I in life? Am I happy? What can I do with and for the people in my life?* I feel like my parents gave me this gift of caring through their example. As I get older, it occurs to me more often that it's all about looking for satisfying ways to live your life and help the people you love live their lives happily as well.

But for anybody getting older (and we all are . . .), it's challenging to do so within a society that is biased against aging. In her memoir *Prime Time,* the great actress Jane Fonda (82 and still an icon) writes that we're operating within a system that has surpassed its usefulness: "Our culture has not come to grips with the ways the longevity revolution has altered our lives. Institutionally, so much of how we do things is the same as it was early in the twentieth century, with our lives segregated into age specific silos: during the first third we learn, during the second third we produce, and the last third we presumably spend on leisure."

Fonda argues that we need to dismantle this structure, describing a new approach in which learning, producing and leisure are integrated through the decades "like a symphony with echoes of different times recurring with slight modifications as in music across the life arc." But she also argues that this integration has not happened yet, that we "don't have the sheet music to this new symphony," and she poses it as the boomers' pioneering challenge: "to compose together a template for how to maximize the potential of this amazing gift of time, so as to become whole, fully realized people over the longer life arc."

I think the struggles of aging are something that we only realize as we are forced by society to bump up against them, when we start to realize that others see us through the stereotype of our age and maybe that we've been doing the same disservice to others. Neither is a very pleasant realization. In *Disrupt Aging: The Bold New Path To Living Your Best Life At Every Age*, JoAnn Jenkins, CEO of AARP writes: "I want people to define me by who I am, not how old I am, and I refuse to allow the old expectations of what I should or should not do at a certain age define what I am going to do. I feel good about where I am in life and I bet you do, too. So instead of just accepting and perpetuating the stereotypes or apologizing for our age—or denying it—let's embrace our age and make the most of it, shall we?"

Shall we, indeed! Jenkins's plan, as she articulates it in the book (and in the title), is to disrupt aging, so that we force those who would override individuals in favour of a stereotype to reckon with the real people behind the age groups. "We need to disrupt aging to help people confront their challenges and embrace their opportunities to the fullest extent possible. That requires changing the way we talk about aging from something we fear to something we look forward to," she says.

For anybody who is now the age that they used to think of as old in the past, we know that most assumptions we made back then are untrue. Sure, there may be a few more aches and pains, but who doesn't hear the same voice in their head as they did when they were 20 years old? Maybe with a bit more wisdom, but you're still yourself.

Aging is like this moving goal post. When we're 20, we think of 40 as old. When we're 40, we think of 65 as old. When we've done focus groups for HomeEquity Bank, we've learned that the stereotype of "older" is to imagine old age as people hunching over and walking with a cane. But even when we do focus groups with people in their eighties, they still don't think of themselves as older. They're all just young at heart.

Ageism is one of the last remaining acceptable "isms." We hear in the workplace that older people are less up-to-date with technology and slower to catch on to new routines. But there are older people who do so much with technology. Our clients prove this with their remarkable uptake of our online information in recent years. There's also been long-standing ageism in real estate. We've heard people grumble about older people blocking the market, that they need to make room for younger people to move in. This is not only unfair but unacceptable. Older people deserve respect. The housing crisis is not the older person's problem to solve.

So, how can we help older people age fabulously? Pondering this topic, I think there are things that older people can do for themselves, things that supporters can do for older people, and definitely things that society and social structures such as government can do.

PAT NODDIN, THE "SKATING GRANDMA," GETS THE SURPRISE OF A LIFETIME

Skating grandma Pat Noddin takes to the ice with her idol, Canadian champion figure skater Kurt Browning.

Throughout this book, we've highlighted the voices of both our clients and our excellent employees. And both Steven and I have also noted how we've grown to love working with the 55-plus demographic. Regardless of whether they're clients, getting to know people in this age range has been a privilege. There's no question that spending time with older adults is the most rewarding aspect of our work at HomeEquity, which leads me to one more story I want to tell you. This person isn't a client, but it is a story of surprise and delight. We even made a video about it at www.youtube.com/watch?v=PRWFhasFsl8.

I first learned about Pat Noddin when I saw her message on Facebook in 2016: "Have met Donald Jackson but haven't met Kurt—so that is going to be my goal, to meet Kurt. I am 80 years old and am an adult skater and have competed in all 13 Canadian Adult Championships. If I were ever granted a wish, it would be to skate one round with Kurt Browning, Elvis and Brian Orser before my body won't allow me to skate anymore . . . an old woman's dream."

Pat is a remarkable woman. After putting down her figure skates in her twenties to take up a life that would include getting married, raising three children and basically getting caught up in the whirl-wind of regular living, this Moncton, New Brunswick, resident did what few others do: she picked up her figure skates again at 58. In 2016, when she posted her wish, she was 79. For those who don't know figure skating, Kurt Browning is a four-time world champion and a four-time Canadian national champion, and Donald Jackson holds four Canadian titles and a bronze medal in the 1960 Winter Olympics. Kurt Browning is an ambassador for HomeEquity Bank, he really believes in our product. After doing an online search to find out more about Pat, I discovered that she was an inspiration to many older Canadians for picking up her skates later in life. So, we thought, why not take action to make some introductions for the one that people already called the "skating grandma?"

I'll let Pat take it from here:

This experience was absolutely a total surprise. I just had no idea. Turns out my whole family was in on it. Even my grandkids knew. I was told that there was a skating event for adult women that I'd been selected to join. My skating coach at the time said she'd put my name in. She said, "pack an overnight bag, pack your skates." We got on the plane at four o'clock in the afternoon. We stayed in Toronto overnight, and the next morning I noticed that my coach was texting somebody.

So, we get in the car. Yvonne came to pick us up the next morning and she was asking me all kinds of questions about my life. I was assuming that her daughters were into figure skating and she was ready to get heavily involved in figure skating, too.

When we got to the Granite Club, they made sure that they pushed me through the dressing room door first. I opened the door and I thought, "Oh my God." I looked at Brian. I looked at Kurt. I looked at Don Jackson. And I said, "I've got to sit down." It was a complete surprise. It was the best experience of my life. They're fabulous people. Coming from small-town Moncton, New Brunswick? They're our idols.

I put my note on Facebook after watching the duet that Kurt and Don had performed for Stars on Ice in May 2016, choreographed for HomeEquity Bank. Somebody had taken a video on their phone. And I thought, it would make this old gal's dream come true if I could have one skate around the rink with them.

It was the best experience ever. I think about it often and I look at the picture. Something in the stars were just lined up the right way to make that happen. I'm one lucky woman.

Since picking up her skates again at age 58 and retraining alongside six-year-olds in the beginner classes, Pat Noddin has gone on to compete in skating contests nationally and internationally. In 2019, she broke her hip but was back on the ice after five months' recovery. In 2020, she turned 84 and is still skating.

THINGS OLDER PEOPLE CAN DO FOR THEMSELVES

I would say one of the most important things you can do is to speak out against stereotypes when you see them. At this point, society has so forcefully marginalized older people that they begin to internalize their own marginalization! They start to feel like they don't have a voice or that their voice is not important. One way that older people can help in this struggle is to give themselves permission to speak up and tell those around them what they want and need. That goes from creating a dialogue with your adult children and letting them know when you need help, to public advocacy for your own age group. Groups like AARP and the Canadian CARP (notably both now known by a simple acronym to remove the retirement aspect from membership) have long advocated for issues of importance to older people. Join one or look online to find out about the issues relevant to you.

Connect with your Members of Parliament when legislation is proposed that threatens to impinge on the rights of older people. Or talk to younger people and get them engaged with issues related to aging. Get involved in advocating for the improvements in Canada's long-term care facilities that are being promised by our governments. If you see these plans getting derailed or bogged down by red tape, hold politicians and health care providers accountable for it.

Keep your own life in as tip-top shape as you can. In talking to experts for this book and through the course of my work at

HomeEquity Bank, I've come to realize that some older people have a lot of inertia or avoidance when it comes to taking action to help themselves. If you've noticed yourself becoming more sedentary or stiff, take action now to prevent yourself from falling into decline. Even a short walk daily or some gentle stretches can help. Make sure you're eating good food and maintaining your social life.

Look for places in your life that cause you stress and see if there's anything you can do to improve them. Often when clients come to us to inquire about a reverse mortgage, they have waited much longer than they needed to in order to find relief. Whether it be shame or indecision or just inertia, that waiting has often taken them to a stressful place. Some even have developed health problems as a result! Even taking a small action, like doing some initial research to find out about your financial options, is a good first step that eventually leads to a better place. I sometimes say inertia is the biggest competitor to our reverse mortgage product. Once people finally take the time to get creative and think about how change can happen for them, new creative solutions flow from that, too. And we're here to help solve the money part.

Continue to plan in your young-old age for your middle-old age and your old-old age. Look at your finances to make sure they will last for your whole life (maybe you will become one of the eleven thousand–plus Canadian centenarians!). If you need to make adjustments, plan and brainstorm now, not when you are in crisis. Think about what you will do when you need more help in your home. Are there modifications you could make now that will help you in the future? If you have any medical conditions, how could they progress down the road and how can you make plans now to help your future self cope? And for goodness sake, plan some fun things, too—what new hobbies or activities could you try out that will make your coming years even more exciting?

THINGS ADULT CHILDREN CAN DO FOR THEIR PARENTS

I considered making this heading "Things Adults Can Do for Older Adults," as that's who these tips really apply to, anyone—except young children, maybe. As is the case with other *isms*, children don't really see aging as a problem. Grandchildren love to hang out with their grandparents, revelling in the attention of the next closest person in their world besides than their parents. And, of course, it doesn't hurt that grandparents spoil their grandchildren rotten (as they should!).

I think one way of reducing ageism is to have better mingling of different ages. People need to spend more time with older people. One way that stereotypes of any kind survive is when people base their knowledge of a group on what they see on TV or from a distance. If more people spent time with their older relatives, they would get to know them as individual personalities, not a vague group they can lump together as "old."

For my part, I regret not spending more time with my maternal grandmother, who passed away at age 93. She was born in 1917 in rural Poland, the only girl in a family with six brothers. As the only girl, she was expected to look after her parents, but at the mature age of 16 she went to the city to attend school. She was fiercely independent: she just knew what she wanted for herself, and that was to get married and have a family of her own. She had four children. One of her daughters died during World War II, and the other three all became well-educated and did well in life. She lived through the Second World War and had life smarts beyond what many others have, even those with impressive educational credentials.

My grandmother was always down-to-earth and very hard-working. She learned to make her own clothes so she could wear pretty things. She was really into natural medicine and made concoctions from herbs and flowers. I remember she even used to bathe in them, so her bathtub was green and brown! We used to go over to her house, where she had a little garden and a chicken coop. She made homemade pasta and the best pierogi. Even though I regret not spending more time with her as an adult, the memories just flow when I think about her, so it's clear that she had more influence on me than I once realized.

These days, I'm enjoying spending time with my uncle and aunt who helped me immigrate to Canada, and my mother-in-law. My uncle and aunt live in Belleville, Ontario—they retired comfortably in their mid-sixties and are now enjoying their best years exploring nearby Prince Edward County and everything it has to offer. We visit them often in the summer to make sure my daughters remain close to them. They love spending time together, and Helen has been learning to sail over the past few summers.

The girls also love spending time with my mother-in-law, who is in her early eighties, and our frequent visits make me feel really close to her. We don't do anything extraordinary beyond Friday and Sunday dinners, which occasionally include singing and dancing, trips down the memory lane, or just visits and lunches on the patio, but it's gratifying to get to know her as a person. She can teach me and the girls so much so effortlessly. Both Sophie and Helen adore her and are always trying to learn new complex words to beat her at *Scrabble*. I see such incredible value in her generation, people with so much storied and lived knowledge. Connecting with older people also makes us think more deeply about our own lives and inspires us with ideas of things we could do.

Neuroscientist Dr. Daniel Levitin, author of the outstanding book *Successful Aging: A Neuroscientist Explores the Power and Potential of Our Lives*, writes in his Introduction about his own mid-eighty-year-old parents, describing them: "as engaged with life as they have ever been." He writes further about the mindset that he observes in them at their age, where despite certain faculties slowing, extraordinary compensating mechanisms, such as having a positive outlook, have kicked in. "Older minds might process information more slowly than younger ones," writes Levitin, "but they can intuitively synthesize a lifetime of information and make smarter decisions based on decades of learning from their mistakes," adding that age also brings many advantages. "They are less fearful of calamities because they've been dealt a few in the past and managed to work through them. Resilience—both their own and each other's—is something they know they can count on."

Levitin's descriptions of his parents are wonderful for the ways in which they make clear that he sees them as people, not just octogenarians. Seeing your own parents as people, spending time with them and asking about their life stories, can help to make the bond you have with them even deeper. At the same time, looking out for them can also help them to live longer and better lives. Be vigilant for any signs that things are going wrong in their lives. It depends on how frequently you see them—if once a year, then you don't want to launch into a financial or lifestyle review as soon as you get in the door. But you could ask a gentle question if you see if bills are piling up. Maybe they forgot their online passwords and need to go to the bank. It doesn't have to be a huge conversation, just a simple "Do you need help with that?"

Vigilance can also extend to keeping an eye on your parents' home. For example, if you see minor repairs needed, that could be another good segue for a conversation. Nobody knows their house better than an adult child, especially if they've spent time growing up in it or even visiting over the years. Ask your parents if it's a case of not being able to find a tradesperson or if they're worried about affording the repairs. If it's a matter of finding people, you can offer to help them get quotes. But don't just go and make the repairs yourself without asking—doing so is a step backwards, infantilizing adults who have taken care of themselves their entire lives.

Another way to get parents to open up is to be vulnerable yourself. After all, that's what builds strong relationships, the ability to trust and confide in one another. Don't expect your parents to share if you don't. Sometimes the best ways to get a dialogue going is to share something that you've been working on yourself and ask for advice. Opening up and being vulnerable is key.

The pandemic has brought on some new elements to worry about, and a good opportunity to ask questions. If you see the contents of your parents' fridge dwindling, ask if they're nervous about going out to shop, and if so, maybe you can introduce them to new solutions, whether it be ordering online or adding their list to your weekly shop. They might also fear going to the bank, so offering to set up online banking could be a good helping hand.

The pandemic has been a challenging time socially, so ask if they are seeing their friends or at least calling. Offer to set them up with videoconferencing services, or if they're already using them with you, offer to set them up with other friends so they can keep their social circle strong. Facing some of these issues together and sharing what's worked for you can make aging parents feel less like they are bothering you by asking for help.

If you're not close enough to your parents to see them regularly (mine are in Poland with a six-hour time difference!), then it's a bit more challenging but still doable. I find even a slight change in people's voices can alert you to something changing in their lives. Making a point to check in regularly (I connect with my parents twice a week using the WhatsApp or Skype platforms) means that you don't need to do a big, long catch-up every time. When it's a busy week, sometimes I even will call my mom from my car, when I have 15 minutes to get from point A to point

B, just to maintain that sense of connection. Calling on special occasions like birthdays can also be a big deal, especially when you take into account how much attention this generation pays to the tradition of special holidays. Sending cards or planning something special shows you care.

THINGS HOMEEQUITY BANK IS DOING FOR OLDER PEOPLE

Steven Ranson and Yvonne Ziomecki at the Equity Release Summit in London, UK, in March 2020.

Before coming to HomeEquity Bank, I had never imagined myself working for a particular age group, let alone the 55-plus group. Now I can hardly see myself working for any other demographic! Meeting so many clients over the years, hearing their stories and especially being able to make a difference in their lives by getting them out of financial difficulty, has been my honour.

Now that I'm enmeshed with this demographic, I see it as part of my job to help educate people about them, to increase their visibility and even to become their advocate. I have commissioned many surveys of our older demographic on topics from debt to downsizing to pesky real estate agents. We have done market research on senior stereotypes and commissioned TV commercials that help poke fun at some of the ones relevant to our business.

Along with every single person at HomeEquity Bank, I've helped to try to explain, simplify, demystify and promote the reverse mortgage product. As you will have read in the Q&As with some of my colleagues, we all really believe that this product works exceptionally well for the right person, and frankly, we're all a little frustrated about how the myths about it persist, in the public sphere and even in banking circles. We're not expecting it to become the most common product on the shelf, but we are hoping that people start to think about it as neutrally as they think of options like lines of credit.

With the rise in home values and decline in pension plans (and throw in a recession or two) that I mentioned in the opening chapter, the reverse mortgage really is a product whose time has come. I sometimes wonder if we launched too early, since we've been in business for over 30 years. Truly it's today that the product is needed. The good thing now is that we've had 30 years of experience, so we know what we're doing! We're the experts. If other banks pop into this market, we get to be the wise old grandparent company (sort of an appropriate persona). As a larger problem, we also wish that some of the unnecessary stigma around debt would disappear. I think the only way that can happen is if we normalize and neutralize financial conversations.

POINT OF PRIDE: OUR DIGITAL POPPY CAMPAIGN

As a company, we're super proud to partner on inspiring initiatives. In 2019, HomeEquity Bank and our advertising agency, Zulu Alpha Kilo Inc., engaged a new generation of supporters for the Royal Canadian Legion, a Canadian organization that supports military veterans. We created a Digital Poppy campaign!

Yvonne Ziomecki and Steven Ranson celebrate the launch of HomeEquity Bank's Digital Poppy campaign in Ottawa.

The Digital Poppy, available at www.MyPoppy.ca, complements the traditional lapel poppy that millions of Canadians wear each year from the last Friday in October to Remembrance Day on November 11. The Digital Poppy can be personalized and dedicated to anyone who served, and then shared on social media. Even at the program's launch in 2019, we managed to gain nearly seven million social impressions and led Digital Poppy purchases from a staggering 114 countries. All funds raised through MyPoppy.ca are directed to the Legion's Poppy Fund, which provides a variety of services to veterans and their families at no cost across the country.

We also created a national TV ad featuring one of Canada's oldest living veterans, Private (Ret'd) Ardwell "Art" Eyres. The ad shows Eyres, helped by his granddaughter, as he dedicates a Digital Poppy to his friend and mentor, Sergeant Major John Copeland.

Finally, we recruited top gamers on Twitch, the world's most popular video game streaming service, known for playing games that glorify war. We invited them to post a message on their streams asking viewers to hold an online moment of silence under the hashtag #PauseToRemember that war is not a game and linking MyPoppy. ca to support veterans by purchasing a Digital Poppy. This innovative campaign not only supported the Royal Canadian Legion but also produced an unprecedented number of marketing awards for HomeEquity Bank.

That year at the One Club for Creativity's annual One Show awards—regarded as one of the most coveted global awards in the creative industry—the campaign took home a Silver Pencil in the livestream category and also a Bronze Pencil in the influencer marketing/single channel category. The campaign also won Gold in the category "Creativity for positive impact: collaboration/partnerships" at New York Festivals AME Awards. Closer to home, *Strategy Magazine*, Canada's leading marketing and advertising publication, awarded the Digital Poppy campaign Gold in the PR: community building category and Gold in the digital games category. Last but not least, the campaign was recognized by the Canadian Marketing Association in the category of Innovative Media - Social Causes.

You can watch the campaign video and all of HomeEquity Bank's videos and commercials on our YouTube channel. There you will find our commercials with Kurt Browning, a series of videos titled "Catch the Scam" featuring the one and only Frank Abagnale Jr., customer testimonials and other video resources.

On a larger scale, I'm just going to go ahead and take credit for HomeEquity Bank's reverse mortgage as a tool that helps facilitate the trend to age in place in Canada. One reason I really respect gerontologist Dr. Sinha is that he's trying to sound the alarm about ageism, when few others give it their due. His examples of other countries like Denmark, which have developed a more community-centred approach to aging, shows that it's definitely possible and decidedly cheaper to support older people who want to stay at home by providing community services and other supports. I love the idea of generating greater support for this option rather than our past approach of thinking of seniors' homes first as a way to support aging parents.

I think we need to keep looking to other countries for insight and guidance on how to bring our services to a similar level. For instance, investing more in public health resources for seniors or creating supports that connect seniors with the rest of the population rather than segregating them because of their age. Growing up in Poland, nobody would ever put their parent in a seniors' home; whereas, in Canada there is a mixture of approaches, influenced by how beautifully complex our country is.

I see aging in place as a route to good aging because it allows you to not only to keep living in the house where you raised your family and developed your community, but also to remain in the neighbourhood where you are comfortable. It seems so unnecessary to disrupt that comfort for no good reason, especially if you can surround yourself with the tools you need to keep living safely in the place you love and where you're able to contribute to the community around you.

LEADERSHIP FOR OLDER CANADIANS

Throughout his decades with the company, HomeEquity Bank President and CEO Steven Ranson has led our organization in its mission to offer greater financial options for Canadians 55 and older. In his work to expand the company's mandate to become a Schedule I bank, Steven has made the reverse mortgage product available to more Canadians. He's also led our support of and our partnership with many organizations devoted to the well-being of older people, from the Royal Canadian Legion to CARP. He's been with the bank since 1997, so he's seen many changes both positive and negative for Canada's aging population.

For my part, I will leave you with a perspective on aging that I think is particularly apt. Daniel Levitin puts it fantastically in *Successful Aging* when he asks and answers this question: "What would it mean for all of us to think of the elderly as resource rather than burden and of aging as culmination rather than denouement? It would mean harnessing a human resource that is being wasted or, at best, underutilized. It would promote stronger family bonds and stronger bonds of friendship among us all. It would mean that important decisions at all scales, from personal matters to international agreements, would be informed by experience and reason, along with the perspective that old age brings. And it might even mean a more compassionate world."

Working for HomeEquity Bank over the years has opened my eyes to all the potential in older people and more. My wish is that older people continue to speak up when they are feeling unseen and to take action when they are unhappy or uncomfortable. I also hope that we as a society are able to move to a place where we are not eyeing their houses, but instead secretly hoping that they age in place as long as they can, so they can retain their status as a vital and integral part of our neighbourhoods and our lives.

AFTERWORD

BY STEVEN RANSON

I hope you enjoyed reading this book on reverse mortgages and other topics including retirement, homeownership, and even safety checklists and gadgets to make aging easier. The most powerful parts of the book for me are the profiles of our customers, both in their own words and through the eyes of our fantastic employees. Each client and their story are unique, and the common thread is how a reverse mortgage can change a life for the better. It can provide additional income, it can relieve the stress of debt payments and it can empower older Canadians to live the retirement they deserve in the home they love. Having joined HomeEquity Bank in 1997, I've spent many years meeting clients and I'm always grateful for the opportunity. I learn a lot from them.

At the beginning of the pandemic, we launched Operation Warm Hug, when we started calling our clients to check up on them to see how they were doing and to let them know they were not alone. My team tasked me with calling the 99- and 100-year-olds, which I thought was incredible! They all had so many stories. Our clients tend to have objectives for how they want to enjoy their retirement. They're really proactive and have a positive outlook on life. They have been through a lot in their lives, and when I spoke with them, they were trying to figure out how to manage through this pandemic. One thing they all told me was how grateful they were to own a house and to be able to stay safe. Their families were dropping off groceries for them, and they were enjoying time on the porch just watching people walk by. Those calls made me nostalgic for something we used to do when the bank was smaller: we would invite clients to lunch once a year to get a chance to meet them, thank them for their business and hear their stories. It used to be a very special event held at The Old Mill in Toronto, and it always left us feeling connected and re-energized, which is exactly how we felt with Operation Warm Hug.

A FEW WORDS ON BETTER ADVOCACY FOR SENIORS

The more I get to know our demographic and their needs, not only financially but in terms of health care, community, social opportunity and other supports, the more I believe we need to take action on their behalf or, where possible, empower older people to take action themselves. Many others have written on this topic before me. In his best-selling book *Successful Aging,* Dr. Daniel Levitin writes:

> The cost of sidelining the elderly is enormous in lost economic and artistic productivity, severed family connections and diminished opportunities. We can begin to model better behaviour by embracing those

who are a generation ahead of us—our parents' generation. And we can adopt practices that will keep us, as older beings, relevant and engaged with others well into our eighties and nineties . . . and perhaps beyond. I argue here for a very different vision of old age, one that sees our final decades as a period of blossoming, a resurgence of life that does not chase after our younger years, but instead embraces the gifts that time can bring.

Another aging advocate, JoAnn Jensen, CEO of AARP, writes that "Corporations, entrepreneurs and small businesses are finally beginning to view the aging population as an opportunity—a growing market for goods and services, a pool of untapped talent and resources, and a driving force behind economic and social innovation—instead of an unaffordable cost and financial burden." These perspectives sum up how we need to start thinking about aging. In Dr. Levitin's case, he argues for a personal awakening whereby we see ourselves and our older age as just part of the journey and not through a lens of decline. Jensen flips the scenario by noting how the general population, and I'd say businesses and service providers in particular, are missing out when they overlook such a powerful demographic.

TO COLLEAGUES IN THE FINANCIAL INDUSTRY

I always say that HomeEquity Bank has a serious advantage in that all we do is reverse mortgages. All we're thinking about is how we can help older Canadians with their financial challenges.

To me, that's a better description of the company than just "the reverse mortgage people." And currently, we're one of the only companies truly serving older people in the financial space.

I think the financial services world is really directed towards younger people. People who are accumulating assets, who the big banks see as much more profitable relationships. Dismissive attitudes towards this demographic suggest that the banks see seniors as people who are winding down their assets or who don't have a lot of assets, and therefore banks aren't looking to serve older people's needs as clients directly. Is that ageism? I don't know, some could say it's just following a bigger opportunity. But I think that the banking world could stand to pay more attention to older people.

When we go out and meet with bankers and brokers, it's surprising how some of them still don't know about our product, or they know something but not enough details to help clients see it as a legitimate choice alongside all the other options. Clearly, they care about these clients, but I don't always see them seeking out new solutions for older people. I think that we in the financial industry could definitely do a better job of looking out for the best interests of our older clients, especially the ones without as many assets.

TO THOSE WHO CAN HELP SENIORS AGE IN PLACE

And what about other services for older people? In the early part of this book, leading gerontologist Dr. Samir Sinha laid out some ways in which other countries have focused on creating community supports for seniors rather than building facilities to house them in. I think aging in place is the way of the future, and I'm not just saying that because it's so compatible with the reverse mortgage product! I call on other businesses to support older people the same way we do. Yes, there are senior discount days at some of our favourite drugstores and movie theatres, but there are more opportunities to serve this demographic in fields from clothing to technology to travel planning.

For adult children of aging parents who are in a position to help support or even guide a decision about aging in place, I urge you to have frank conversations with your parents. If they want to age in place, and our polls show that more than 90 percent do, then look seriously at the supports that are needed to do so. Take a look at the checklists we've included in this book and at the recommendations for other resources on how to make the improvements that will help your parent to live in their home for as long as possible.

Start having those awkward conversations about wills and advanced directives, and even about whether they have enough friends and if they'd like to find out about joining the nearby seniors' centre. Maybe offer to go with them their first time to help them explore a new social opportunity. Find out about supports that can make their lives easier, from setting them up with a regular grocery delivery service to arranging for their lawn care. Do all of it without taking over or hassling them, but rather operating from a place of empathy and compassion. If they're already doing these things, cheer them on!

To businesses that can offer services that would help older people but haven't yet gone after this market, please do! They're great clients. They have lots of stories to tell. Yes, they may take longer to take up some technologies, but they've been around much longer than you have, so practise your patience. The reward of serving older people is that they help enrich our community as a whole.

TO THOSE WHO CAN HELP IMPROVE LONG-TERM CARE FACILITIES

Like all Canadians, I was heartbroken to watch how older Canadians suffered disproportionately in long-term care facilities during the pandemic. What happened to them is inexcusable, and they need to be treated with the dignity and respect they deserve. The fact that in the early stage of the pandemic Canada had the highest percentage of deaths in long-term care and nursing homes compared with other OECD countries is shameful. We owe it to them to do better, and we must do better. It starts with working with our like-minded partners, stakeholders and policy makers in government to find sensible solutions that puts their needs first, and that of their families who are demanding alternatives to the status quo.

That's why I'm a firm believer in making tangible investments in home and community care. Older Canadians should have the choice to age safely in place at home, and it's up to both the public and private sector to develop strategies to make this a reality.

If we're looking for inspiration on how to move this forward, I suggest we turn our attention beyond our borders to learn from other countries who have made home and community care a priority. One of them is Denmark, which has done a remarkable job. The Scandinavian country's strategy has allowed them to avoid building new long-term care beds for almost two decades, resulting in a 20 percent reduction in its long-term care expenditures in the first decade of the initiative. In my view, there is no reason why we can't make similar investments here in Canada.

While there are no copy-and-paste solutions, we should look to the successes of other nations to start having critical conversations about how we can emulate those policies here for the sake of our own citizens.

The reality is, we are up against the clock. As I've said before, boomers make up largest and fastest-growing demographic in this country and as their age goes up, so do costs to help care for them. If we don't act now, we will face a health care crisis on a level never seen before, and this will be felt by everyone, regardless of age. That's why it's so important we prioritize investing in home and community care today before it's too late. While it's no secret that I'm a proponent for supporting programs to help older Canadians age in place, I do realize that long-term care and nursing facilities will be a necessity for many people as well.

TO THOSE WHO CAN HELP PROVIDE MORE OVERSIGHT FOR SENIORS

Even if we wanted to leave them behind, I don't think seniors will let us. In 2019, more than one in six (17.5 percent) Canadians was 65 or over. By 2031, it is projected that this proportion will rise to nearly one in four (23 percent). In *Unretirement: How Baby Boomers Are Changing the Way We Think About Work, Community, and the Good Life*, author Chris Farrell writes that "We're at the early stages of a long, difficult transition towards a different vision of the elder years. In the process, aging boomers will influence for the better how younger generations view their jobs, their careers and their expectations about the mix of work and leisure, engagement and meaning, especially during the last third of life."

I find it particularly exciting that Farrell not only points to boomers leading the charge, but that the change they enact will lead to changes rippling forward. Look at the way that boomers working past the traditional retirement age has already influenced the way that we see this transition. So many articles have been written about boomers rejecting an abrupt and final end to work in favour of a slow tapering where they take on more flexible jobs, sometimes even ones that fit their passions, that allow them to ease into a new life balance. Now that we've seen them model this life, doesn't it seem like something we should all try? What else will these leaders model for us that will turn out to be better than the way we did things before?

But the road is not always easy for these renegades. Those work transitions sound easy, but often they were made in the face of ageism and resistance from employers, and still are. That's why I think that formalizing programs and supports at the government level would help to establish a new dignity for our elders. I'm very excited to read about Dr. Sinha's participation in an advocacy movement by a growing number of Canadians, health and social care professionals, economists, and national organizations who suggest that the time has come for a National Senior Strategy to "build a nation that values, encourages and promotes the wellness and independence of older Canadians."

The National Institute on Ageing website, nationalseniorsstrategy.ca, outlines the movement's five principles of access, equity, choice, value and quality. In its most recent report, *National Seniors Strategy* (Third Edition), released in October 2020, the Institute once again advocates four pillars on which to focus, including independent, productive and engaged citizens; healthy and active lives; care closer to home; and support for caregivers, as an umbrella to address 12 specific policy issues from ageism to poverty to housing to advance care support to workplace support, among others.

Seeing more public advocacy such as this, or the regular output by groups like our partner organization CARP, give me hope that sometime soon we will finally catch up to the demographic that is leading us through these changes, the people that we at HomeEquity Bank are proud to call our clients.

FINAL REMARKS

As we come to the closing few paragraphs, I've been reminded of so many incredible and rewarding experiences at HomeEquity Bank over the past 20 years and I must say I've enjoyed this journey down memory lane. I still pinch myself about how fortunate I am to lead such an incredible organization, filled with caring, hard-working and devoted employees who are as big believers in our products as I am.

The truth is, that's not something that you can find in many companies of our size. But it's a testament to our culture that has helped hundreds of people flourish in their careers, and they've helped make meaningful change in the lives of so many Canadians 55 and older. I can't help but smile about that.

HomeEquity Bank is more than just the CHIP Reverse Mortgage, or the other products we sell. We're a company that provides hope, peace of mind and happiness. I've spoken to literally thousands of customers over the years and they all tell me how thrilled they are to have us in their corner. If it wasn't for their reverse mortgage, life would be a lot different.

It's stories like these that motivate me, and our team, to continue to raise the bar and provide exceptional service to our customers and do our very best to support our communities across the country. Words cannot describe how proud I am about this.

In closing, the main thing I hope our readers take away is that you deserve to be able to enjoy your retirement, your way, in the home you love. You've earned it. And know this: if life ever throws you a curveball, HomeEquity Bank is ready to help take you home. That's a promise we've always made, and it's one we will continue to keep.

Thank you.

President and CEO Steven Ranson celebrates 20 years at HomeEquity Bank with his wife, Sharon, and his children, Maggie and Tom.

SOURCES

FOREWORD

www.trustpilot.com

www.canadianbusiness.com/growth-500-canadas-fastest-growing-companies/

www.theglobeandmail.com/business/rob-magazine/top-growing-companies/

www.ipsos.com/en-ca/news-polls/HomeEquity-Bank-Poll-July-2018

INTRODUCTION

www.globenewswire.com/news-release/2020/03/04/1994809/0/en/Aging-in-
    Place-Report-Reveals-86-of-Urban-Canadian-Baby-Boomers-Older-Adult-
    Homeowners-Want-to-Live-in-their-Homes-for-as-Long-as-Possible.html

www.statcan.gc.ca/eng/subjects-start/seniors_and_aging

omny.fm/shows/640-toronto/playlists/homeequity-bank-retirement-radio-show

CHAPTER ONE

www150.statcan.gc.ca/n1/pub/75-006-x/2019001/article/00012-eng.htm

www.thestar.com/news/canada/2015/03/04/toronto-housing-prices-nearly-
    triple-since-1970s.html

trreb.ca/index.php/news/
    news-releases/1021-trreb-releases-september-resale-housing-report

creastats.crea.ca/en-CA/

SOURCES

www.ratehub.ca/banks/bank-mortgage-rates

www.theglobeandmail.com/real-estate/the-market/remember-when-what-have-we-learned-from-80s-interest-rates/article24398735/

www150.statcan.gc.ca/n1/pub/75-006-x/2019001/article/00005-eng.htm

www12.statcan.gc.ca/census-recensement/2016/dp-pd/dt-td/Rp-eng.cfm?LANG=E&APATH=3&DETAIL=0&DIM=0&FL=A&FREE=0&GC=0&GID=0&GK=0&GRP=1&PID=110581&PRID=10&PTYPE=109445&S=0&SHOWALL=0&SUB=0&Temporal=2017&THEME=121&VID=0&VNAMEE=&VNAMEF=

www150.statcan.gc.ca/n1/pub/11-631-x/11-631-x2016001-eng.htm

www150.statcan.gc.ca/n1/pub/71-222-x/71-222-x2018003-eng.htm

nationalseniorsstrategy.ca/wp-content/uploads/2020/09/NSS_2020_Third_Edition.pdf

www.cbc.ca/news/business/statistics-canada-debt-1.5609510

www150.statcan.gc.ca/n1/daily-quotidien/190619/dq190619f-eng.htm

hoopp.com/docs/default-source/about-hoopp-library/advocacy/the-value-of-a-good-pension-102018.pdf

www.cbc.ca/news/business/retirement-savings-broadbent-institute-1.3450084

cibc.mediaroom.com/2018-02-08-Am-I-saving-enough-to-retire-Vast-majority-of-Canadians-just-dont-know-CIBC-poll

www150.statcan.gc.ca/t1/tbl1/en/tv.action?pid=1310038901

www.canada.ca/en/services/benefits/publicpensions/cpp/cpp-benefit/amount.html

nationalseniorsstrategy.ca/wp-content/uploads/2016/10/National-Seniors-Strategy-Second-Edition.pdf

www.cihi.ca/sites/default/files/document/covid-19-rapid-response-long-term-care-snapshot-en.pdf

www.cihi.ca/en/how-much-will-we-spend-on-health-in-2019

www.fraserinstitute.org/studies/price-of-public-health-care-insurance-2020-edition

www.newswire.ca/news-releases/health-system-failing-to-meet-seniors-needs-canadians-facing-increasing-financial-burden-856904743.html

www.comfortlife.ca/retirement-community-resources/home-care-cost

www.comfortlife.ca/retirement-community-resources/retirement-costs-ontario

trreb.ca/index.php/news/
news-releases/1021-trreb-releases-september-resale-housing-report

CHAPTER TWO

creastats.crea.ca/en-CA/

dx.doi.org/10.2139/ssrn.2528944

www.sauder.ubc.ca/people/thomas-davidoff

CHAPTER THREE

www.statcan.gc.ca/eng/subjects-start/seniors_and_aging

www.activeagingcanada.ca/

www.cihi.ca/sites/default/files/document/covid-19-rapid-response-long-term-
care-snapshot-en.pdf

www150.statcan.gc.ca/n1/daily-quotidien/190930/dq190930a-eng.htm

www.thecanadianencyclopedia.ca/en/article/baby-boom

www150.statcan.gc.ca/n1/pub/91f0015m/2014011/03-eng.htm

www12.statcan.gc.ca/census-recensement/2011/as-sa/98-311-x/98-311-
x2011003_2-eng.cfm

blog.advertising.expedia.com/
canadian_genz_millennials_go_abroad_for_outdoor_exploration

www.homeequitybank.ca/media/press-releases/new-research-calls-out-
unconscious-age-bias-as-boomers-push-back-against-offensive-labels-and-
aging-stereotypes

www.healthyagingpoll.org/report/everyday-ageism-and-health

www.bloomsbury.com/us/unretirement-9781620401576

www.historymuseum.ca/cmc/exhibitions/hist/medicare/medic-2c01e.html

opentextbc.ca/introductiontosociology2ndedition/chapter/
chapter-13-aging-and-the-elderly/

CHAPTER FOUR

www.canada.ca/en/employment-social-development/corporate/seniors/forum/
aging.html

www.Aginginplace.org

careforagingparents.com/

www.penguinrandomhouse.com/books/220576/
how-to-age-in-place-by-mary-a-languirand-phd-and-robert-f-bornstein-phd

www.ipsos.com/en-ca/news-polls/HomeEquity-Bank-Poll-July-2018

www150.statcan.gc.ca/t1/tbl1/en/tv.action?pid=1310038901

www.suzeorman.com/products/
The-Ultimate-Retirement-Guide-for-50-and-Over

cibc.mediaroom.com/2018-02-08-Am-I-saving-enough-to-retire-Vast-majority-
of-Canadians-just-dont-know-CIBC-poll

CHAPTER FIVE

www.thesimpledollar.com/credit/manage-debt/the-emotional-effects-of-debt

www.homeequitybank.ca/media/press-releases/
downsizing-the-home-not-a-guaranteed-financial-windfall-in-retirement/

www.chip.ca/reverse-mortgage-resources/joyce-wayne-retirement-matters/

www.ontario.ca/page/rent-increase-guideline

www150.statcan.gc.ca/n1/pub/11-631-x/11-631-x2016001-eng.htm

www.cmhc-schl.gc.ca/en/housing-observer-online/2020-housing-observer/
results-2020-seniors-housing-survey

www.comfortlife.ca/retirement-community-resources/retirement-costs-ontario

https://elizz.com/planning/cost-of-assisted-living/

www.lyndsaygreen.com

cdn.nar.realtor/sites/default/files/documents/2020-generational-trends-report-03-05-2020.pdf

www.healthyagingpoll.org/report/loneliness-and-health

CHAPTER SIX

cameronhuddleston.com/mom-and-dad-we-need-to-talk

www.homeequitybank.ca/media/press-releases/talking-to-aging-parents-about-finance

www.penguinrandomhouse.ca/books/43853/our-turn-to-parent-by-barbara-dunn-and-linda-scott/9780307357137

www.suzeorman.com/products/The-Ultimate-Retirement-Guide-for-50-and-Over

www.amazon.ca/Retirement-Income-Life-Getting-Without/dp/1988344050

www.canada.ca/en/financial-consumer-agency.html

www.getsmarteraboutmoney.ca

www.moneysense.ca

findependencehub.com

www.theglobeandmail.com/authors/rob-carrick

boomerandecho.com

retirehappy.ca

www.bnnbloomberg.ca/talent/pattie-lovett-reid-1.451950

CHAPTER SEVEN

www.cihi.ca/en/1-in-9-new-long-term-care-residents-potentially-could-have-been-cared-for-at-home

www.cihi.ca/en/falls-and-vehicle-collisions-top-causes-of-injury-hospitalizations-for-seniors

SOURCES

www.penguinrandomhouse.com/books/220576/
   how-to-age-in-place-by-mary-a-languirand-phd-and-robert-f-bornstein-phd/

www.homeequitybank.ca/media/press-releases/seniors-want-to-age-in-place-
   but-study-shows-58-must-renovate-their-home/

midnightscoop.com/

Pinterest.ca

Sources for some of the products noted in the gardening section

Raised planters: www.gardeners.com/buy/vegtrug-trough-planters/8598402VS.
   html?SC=XNET0279#start=28

Ergonomic hand weeder from Lee Valley: www.leevalley.com/en-ca/shop/
   garden/garden-care/weeders/101364-radius-ergonomic-hand-weeder?gclid
   =Cj0KCQiAwP3yBRCkARIsAABGiPo5ouy3-dz2dujEZrArVLftdCLSYfpWYi0hFX-
   0UpS7KoS1pc6uLsPcaAmMcEALw_wcB

Bionic gloves: www.bionicgloves.com/rose_gardening?quantity=1&custcol1=2&
   custcol2=3&custcol3=15&custcol4=3

Folding stool/kneeler: www.leevalley.com/en-ca/shop/garden/garden-care/
   stools/45632-folding-kneeler-stool

www.pcmag.com/news/the-best-smart-home-devices-for-2020

www.thetileapp.com/en-ca

Online adaptive clothing stores

usa.tommy.com/en/tommy-adaptive

www.caringvillage.com/2018/02/12/top-5-adaptive-clothing-companies

Services

www.skipthedishes.com

www.ubereats.com/ca

www.hellofresh.ca

www.makegoodfood.ca

www.uber.com

www.lyft.com

www.fiverr.com

www.taskrabbit.ca/ca/en

www.homecareontario.ca/our-members/list-of-members

www.mealsonwheels.ca

www.canada.ca/seniors

www.youtube.com/watch?v=2CemBNIy6ls&t=1s

antifraudcentre-centreantifraude.ca/index-eng.htm

proaccessibility.ca

Sources for some of the products noted in the kitchen section

www.independentliving.com/category/kitchen-and-cooking-aids/a

www.allegromedical.com/daily-living-aids-c519/kitchen-aids-c3618.html

www.wrightstuff.biz/adaptive-cups-glasses-straws.html

promenaid.com/handrails/grab-bars

www.invisiacollection.com

www.savaria.com

CHAPTER EIGHT

www.janefonda.com/prime-time/

www.aarp.org/disrupt-aging/info-2016/joann-jenkins-disrupt-aging-book.html

www.aarp.org

www.carp.ca

www.penguinrandomhouse.com/books/598506/
successful-aging-by-daniel-j-levitin

www.mypoppy.ca

www.ameawards.com/Winners/
Medalists/8a6bc63a-9af9-43af-9102-5af99112850f

SOURCES

awards.strategyonline.ca/

www.the-cma.org/

www.youtube.com/c/HomeEquityBank/videos

www.youtube.com/watch?v=PRWFhasFsl8

AFTERWORD

www.penguinrandomhouse.com/books/598506/
    successful-aging-by-daniel-j-levitin

www.aarp.org/disrupt-aging/info-2016/joann-jenkins-disrupt-aging-book.html

www150.statcan.gc.ca/n1/daily-quotidien/190930/dq190930a-eng.htm

www.bloomsbury.com/us/unretirement-9781620401576

www.nationalseniorsstrategy.ca

ABOUT THE AUTHORS

STEVEN RANSON, MBA, CPA, CA
PRESIDENT AND CEO, HOMEEQUITY BANK

For more than 20 years, Steven Ranson has been at the helm of HomeEquity Bank, playing a vital role in establishing the company as Canada's leading provider of reverse mortgages. Steve is an inspiring leader and a preeminent Canadian voice in the reverse mortgage industry. He is also a noted commentator on issues that Canadians face as they grow older, both financially and in terms of their overall well-being.

YVONNE ZIOMECKI, MBA
EXECUTIVE VICE PRESIDENT, HOMEEQUITY BANK

Since 2013, Yvonne Ziomecki has been a driving force in introducing reverse mortgages to Canadians as a key tool in structuring a comfortable and financially sound retirement. Her experience helping Canada's fastest-growing demographic has made her a stellar go-to expert in the Canadian media, where she is a frequent contributor on issues including retirement living, fraud education and age-related bias.

automatic ~~jar~~ opener
bag openers
pinterest, ca